.D

THE GOVERNMENTS OF
FRANCE, ITALY, AND GERMANY

BY

A. LAWRENCE LOWELL, LL.D., Ph.D.
President of Harvard University

CAMBRIDGE
HARVARD UNIVERSITY PRESS
LONDON: HUMPHREY MILFORD
OXFORD UNIVERSITY PRESS
1914

PREFACE

THIS volume is an abridgment of the author's *Governments and Parties in Continental Europe,* published in 1897. It has been prepared in order that certain portions of the latter, particularly those dealing with the framework of government in France, Italy and Germany, may be more easily used in college classes.

Some changes have been made in the text, but only where the legislation of the last seventeen years has changed the actual machinery of government. Matters of opinion are left as they were in the original edition.

CONTENTS

CHAPTER I

FRANCE : INSTITUTIONS

	PAGE
Origin and nature of parliamentary government in England	2
The system imperfectly copied on the Continent	6
The French constitutional laws	7
History of their creation	8
The method of amendment	12
Their legal and moral effect	13
The Chamber of Deputies	14
The method of election, *scrutin de liste* and *scrutin d'arrondissement*	15
The Chamber a tumultuous body	18
The Senate	19
Its functions and actual influence	21
The ministers as a rule not responsible to it	22
The National Assembly	26
The President of the Republic	26
His functions	27
His powers really exercised by responsible ministers	28
The Council of State	30
The ministers	32
Their responsibility to the Chamber of Deputies	33
Their enormous power (which is due to the four following matters)	33
The paternal nature of the government	34
The centralization of local government	36
The department, with its prefect and general council	36
The arrondissement and the canton	40
The commune, with its mayor and communal council	40
Paris and Lyons	42
The legislative powers of the executive	43
Ordinances and appropriations	44

CONTENTS

The judicial powers of the executive 47
 Difference between English and French history . . . 47
  In England the royal power grew early and took a judicial form 48
  In France it developed late and took an administrative form 51
 Effect of the doctrine of the separation of powers . . . 54
  Questions of the legality of official acts withdrawn from the ordinary courts 55
  The administrative courts and the court of conflicts . 57
 The state of siege 63
Effect of the French system on the position of the ministers . 64
Note on Gneist's views on English and French history . . . 65

CHAPTER II

FRANCE : PARTIES

The influence of parties in popular government 69
The parliamentary system normally produces two parties . . 70
 It cannot work well otherwise 72
In France there are many parties or groups 74
Causes of the subdivision of parties 76
 Lack of a political consensus 76
 Theoretical character of French political opinions . . . 81
 Lack of the habit of political organization 82
 The election of the deputies by majority vote . . . 84
 The system of committees in the Chambers 87
  This undermines the authority of the cabinet and its ability to hold the majority together 90
 The use of interpellations 93
  This has a similar effect 94
  It is due to jealousy of the ministers 100
Results of the subdivision of parties 103
 A change of ministry does not mean change of party . . 103
 The cabinets short-lived 104
 As a rule they are coalitions and therefore weak . . . 105
 They must confer favors on the deputies to win votes . . 106
 The deputies in turn must curry favor with the local nominating committees and the constituents 108
Prospects of the Republic 113
 Since the Revolution there has been no change of the party in power without a revolution 114
 Possible organic changes 117

CHAPTER III

ITALY : INSTITUTIONS

The formation of the kingdom 120
The Statuto 122
The King 126
The ministers 127
The Senate 128
The Chamber of Deputies 130
    The franchise, the method of election, etc. 131
The administrative system 135
    The ordinance power 139
    The civil service 140
Local government 142
The judicial system 144
    The courts and the officials 145
    Administrative law and the administrative courts . . . 147
    Weakness of the judicial system 150
The church 152
    The doctrine of a free church in a free state . . . 153
    The monastic orders 155
    The Pope, and the law of the Papal Guarantees . . . 157
    Embarrassing situation of the Vatican 159

CHAPTER IV

GERMANY : THE STRUCTURE OF THE EMPIRE

The Holy Roman Empire 164
The growth of Prussia 165
The Germanic Confederation and the Diet 166
The failure of the Liberal attempt at union in 1848–49 . . 168
Bismarck and the war of 1866 171
The North German Confederation and the Empire . . . 172
The constitution 174
Nature of the federal union 175
    Legislative centralization and executive decentralization . . 175
    Inequality of rights among the members 178
        The privileges of Prussia 178
        The privileges of the other states 181
The Reichstag : its composition 184
    Its powers 188

The Bundesrath : its composition 191
   Its character and the position of the members . . . 194
   Its internal organization 197
   Its powers and privileges 199
   Its actual influence 204
The Emperor 205
   Interlacing of his powers as Emperor and as King of Prussia . 207
The Chancellor 208
   He is not responsible to the Reichstag 210
   His functions and substitutes 211
The judicial system : The Reichsgericht 213
   Power of the courts to hold statutes unconstitutional . . 214
General character of the federal system 216

THE GOVERNMENTS OF FRANCE, ITALY, AND GERMANY

FRANCE

THE GOVERNMENTS OF
FRANCE, ITALY, AND GERMANY

CHAPTER I.

FRANCE: INSTITUTIONS.

In order to understand the government of a country it is not enough to know the bare structure of its institutions. It is necessary to follow the course of politics; to inquire how far the various public bodies exercise the authority legally vested in them; and to try to discover the real sources of power. It is necessary, in short, to study the actual working of the system; and although this depends chiefly upon the character, the habits, and the traditions of the people, it is also influenced in no small measure by details, like the method of voting, the procedure in the legislative chambers, and other matters, that are too often overlooked on account of their apparent insignificance. Now in several of the states on the Continent of Europe the main features of representative government have been copied directly or indirectly from English models, while the details have grown up of themselves, or are a survival from earlier tradition. It is not surprising, therefore, that the two are more or less inconsistent with each other, and that this want of harmony has had a pronounced effect on public life.

Although most people to-day are familiar with the

Parliament-
ary govern-
ment in
England.

parliamentary system of government as it has developed in England, it may not be out of place to give a brief description of it here on account of the profound influence it has had in other countries.

The Middle Ages gave birth to two political ideas. The first of these was a division of the people into separate classes or estates, each of which had independent political functions of its own. The second was representative government, or the election — by those estates whose members were too numerous to assemble in a body — of deputies authorized to meet together and act for the whole estate. The number of these estates, and the number of separate chambers in which their representatives sat, varied in the different countries of Europe;[1] but it so happened that in England all the political power of the estates became in time vested in two chambers.[2] One of them, the House of Lords, contained the whole body of peers, who were the

---

[1] Thus in France, and in most continental countries, there were three, while in Sweden there were four : the clergy, the nobles, the cities, and the peasants. The existence of only two Houses in England might almost be called an accident. (Cf. Freeman, *Growth of the English Constitution*, p. 93.)

[2] In 1664 Convocation, which was the ecclesiastical chamber, discontinued the practice of voting separate taxes on the clergy, and thus the clergy definitely ceased to be an estate of the realm. (See Hallam, *Const. Hist. of England*, chap. xvi.)

successors of the great feudal vassals of the Crown; while the other, the House of Commons, was composed of the deputies from the towns and counties, who had gradually consolidated into a single house, and might be said to represent all the people who were not peers.

By degrees the House of Commons acquired the right of originating all bills for raising or spending money, and hence its support became essential to the Crown.   But its members were independent, and on the whole less open to court influence than the peers. They felt under no obligation to support the policy of the government, or to vote an appropriation unless they understood and approved the purpose for which it was to be used; and King William III., during his wars with France, found them by no means as easy to manage as he could wish.   Hitherto his ministers had been selected from both political parties, and hence were not in harmony with each other, and were unable to exert an effective influence in Parliament; but between 1693 and 1696 he dismissed the Tories, and confided all the great offices of state to the Whigs, who had a majority in the Commons.   The result was that the House which had been turbulent became docile; and the ministers by winning its confidence were able to guide it, and obtain the appropriations that were required.   This was the origin of the practice of selecting the ministers from the leaders of the majority in Parliament, — a practice which at a later time crystallized into a principle of the British Constitution.[1]   But of course men who held the most important offices, and at the same time led the

[1] Macaulay, *History of England*, chap. xx.

House of Commons, were certain not to be mere tools in the hands of the King. They were sure to try to carry out their own policy, and when the sceptre of William had passed into the hands of the first two Georges, who were foreigners and took little interest in English politics, the ministers exercised the royal power as they pleased, and became in fact the custodians of the prerogatives of the Crown. The subordination of the King to his ministers is, indeed, the inevitable result of the system; for so long as the latter retain their influence over the House, and can direct its votes, they can hold their offices and administer them according to their own views. If the King attempts to dismiss them they can block the wheels of government, by inducing Parliament to withhold supplies; and if, on the other hand, they cease to be the leaders of the House, and a different party with new leaders gets a majority, the King finds himself obliged to send for these and intrust the government to them. The system which had been devised in order that the King might control the House of Commons became, therefore, the means by which the House of Commons, through its leaders, controlled the King, and thus all the power of the House of Commons and of the Crown became vested in the same men, who guided legislation and took charge of the administration at the same time.

The House of Lords, meanwhile, was losing ground. It had no right to initiate or amend money bills, and, what was far more important, it had no influence on the formation or the policy of the cabinet. The ministers were, indeed, often peers, but they were not selected because they belonged to the majority in the House of Lords, nor did they resign when that body voted against them. Like their colleagues from the other House, they represented the majority in the Commons, and were solidly in accord with it. The House of Lords, therefore, found itself confronted by the combined power of the Crown and the House of Commons, and this it was unable to resist. In fact the power to create new peers furnished the Crown, or rather the ministers acting in its name, with a weapon always ready to break an obstinate resistance, and at the time of the Reform Bill of 1832 a threat of this kind was enough to compel submission. The Upper House has thus gradually lost authority, until now it does not venture to reject any measure on which the cabinet is really in earnest, — unless perchance, as in the case of the recent Home Rule bill, it is convinced that the House of Commons does not fairly represent the people, and that a new election would result in a victory for the party in opposition. In such a case the refusal to pass the measure is tantamount to a demand for a Referendum.[1]

The ministers remain in office only so long as they continue to be the leaders of the Lower House and are able to control the majority. When this condition has changed, a vote is sometimes passed to the effect that the ministers have ceased to possess the confidence of the House; but such an express declaration is rarely used

[1] It is a curious fact that the Premier of New South Wales has recently proposed to prevent deadlocks between the Houses by providing that after a bill has been rejected once by the Legislative Council and again passed by the Assembly, the Council shall not have power to reject it a second time, but may require it to be submitted to popular vote. A similar proposal has been discussed in Belgium.

at the present day, and a hostile vote on any matter of considerable importance is treated as a proof that the government has no longer the support of a majority. After such a vote, therefore, the ministers resign, and if there is a normal division into two parties the Crown sends for the leader of the opposition, and intrusts him with the formation of a cabinet. The defeated ministers have, however, one other alternative. If they think that the House of Commons has ceased to be in harmony with the opinion of the nation, they can dissolve Parliament in the name of the Crown, and try the chance of a new election. Thus in the English parliamentary system the direction of the legislature, and the control of the executive, is in the hands of the leaders of the majority in the House of Commons. For their exercise of power these leaders are directly responsible to the House of Commons, which can call them to account at any time; while the House itself is responsible to the people, which gives its verdict whenever the end of the term of Parliament or a dissolution brings about a general election.

Turning now from the consideration of English forms of government to those in use on the Continent, we find that the main features of the British Constitution have been very generally imitated. In fact, the plan of two chambers, one of which issues from an extended suffrage and has the primary control of the purse, and of a cabinet whose members appear in the chambers and are jointly responsible to the more popular one, so that all the ministers resign on an adverse vote of that chamber, is of Eng-

Parliamentary government on the Continent.

lish origin, and has spread widely over Europe. These features of the parliamentary system are striking, and have become famous, while the procedure in the House of Commons, which enables the system to work smoothly, has attracted far less attention, and has been followed very little. This is peculiarly true of France, where the principle of cabinet responsibility has been adopted to the fullest extent, but where there exist at the same time several practices that help to twist parliamentary government out of the normal form. More curious still is the fact that these very practices have been blindly copied by other countries which intended to imitate the English system.

A description of the French government must begin with its structure, with the legal composition and powers of the different political bodies. This will occupy the present chapter. In the next, the actual working of the system will be considered, especially in regard to the character of political parties; and an attempt will be made to explain the peculiarities that are found by a reference to the condition of the people, and to those parts of the political machinery that seem to have a marked effect. In other words, we shall begin with the skeleton, and then take up the muscles and nerves. *Outline of the first and second chapters.*

The first thing one looks for in a modern government is the constitution; but although the French Republic has a constitution, it differs in two very important respects from those to which we are accustomed. It is not comprised in any one document, but in a series of distinct laws, and it *The French Constitution.*

contains few provisions limiting the functions of the different bodies, or prescribing fundamental rights which the state is enjoined to respect. This is a departure not only from American, but also from the earlier French usage, for previous constitutions in France have been long documents and have contained elaborate bills of rights; although the absence of practical guarantees has made their effectiveness depend upon the good pleasure of the government. The present constitution is very different, and barely provides for the organization of the powers of the state, without even speaking of such important matters as a yearly budget or the tenure of office of the judges. It does little more than establish the main framework of the government by declaring what the chief organs of public life shall be, leaving them almost entirely free to exercise their authority as they see fit. The reason for such a departure from French traditions is to be found in the circumstances of the case. The earlier constitutions in France were attempts to frame an ideal system, but the present one resulted from an immediate need of providing a regular government of some sort that could rule the country for the time, and was drawn up by men who had no belief in its inherent perfection. To understand this it is necessary to glance at the history of the period.

The rapid series of defeats suffered by the French armies at the hands of the Germans, in 1870, destroyed the tottering authority of the empire, and as soon as the news of the surrender of Napoleon III. at Sedan reached Paris an insurrection

History of its creation.

broke out on the fourth of September. The republic was at once proclaimed, but this was no time to debate plans for a constitution, and so long as the war lasted the country was ruled by the self-elected Government of the National Defense. When the war was over, a National Assembly with indefinite powers was chosen by universal suffrage. The member of this body who commanded the most general public confidence was Thiers, the historian, and former minister of Louis Philippe. To him the Assembly intrusted the executive power, and in August, 1871, it gave him the title of President, without, however, fixing any term for the duration of the office. Thiers was constantly urged to introduce the parliamentary system by allowing his ministers to assume the responsibility for his acts, but this he refused to do, saying that the position in which it would place him, although perfectly consistent with the dignity of an hereditary king, was for him, a little *bourgeois*, entirely out of the question.[1] He held himself, however, personally responsible to the Assembly for the conduct of his government, took part in the debates on the measures he proposed, and declared that he was ready to resign at any time, if the majority wanted him to do so.[2] This state of things continued

[1] The law of Aug. 31, 1871, declared that the President as well as the ministers should be responsible to the Assembly. See Dupriez, *Les Ministres dans les Principaux Pays d'Europe et d'Amérique*, vol. ii. p. 320.

[2] The law of March 13, 1873, abolished the right of the President to take part in debate, and while allowing him to address the Assembly, ordered the sitting to be suspended immediately after his speech. This was, of course, an attempt to reduce the personal influence of Thiers, (Dupriez, vol. ii. pp. 321–22.)

for nearly two years, when a hostile vote forced Thiers to retire. His successor, Marshal MacMahon, was elected for a term of seven years, and as the new President was not a member of the Assembly, his cabinet became responsible in the parliamentary sense. But although the chief magistrate now held office for a fixed period, and was freed from the caprices of an uncertain majority, still there was no constitution and no permanent organization of the government. The situation was, in fact, a provisional one, prolonged abnormally by the strange condition of politics. The monarchists formed a majority of the Assembly, but they were hopelessly divided into two sections, — the Legitimists, whose candidate was the Comte de Chambord, and the Orleanists, who followed the Comte de Paris. At one moment it seemed not impossible that the Comte de Chambord might become king, and some of his supporters opened negotiations for the purpose ; but these were brought to nothing by obstinacy of the Prince himself, who was a true scion of his race, and would not yield one jot of his pretensions. He even refused to accept the tricolor flag that means so much to Frenchmen, and clung doggedly to the ancient white standard of his house. Under such circumstances, a monarchy was out of the question, and so this assembly The Constitu- of monarchists at last set to work to organize tional Laws. a republic ; or rather a sufficient number of monarchists, feeling that a republic was, for the time at least, inevitable, joined with the minority to establish a government on the only basis possible.[1] But

---

[1] Very good brief descriptions of the formation of the Constitution

although the republican form was adopted, the institutions that were set up departed essentially from the ideas which the French had been accustomed to associate with that term. The present government, like all political systems that have been created suddenly and have proved lasting, was essentially a compromise. From the French republican principles there was borrowed, besides the name, little more than the election of the chief magistrate, while from the traditions of constitutional monarchy were taken the irresponsibility of the head of the state, and the existence of a second legislative chamber.[1] Now it was natural that no one should feel inclined to construct an ideal system on a hybrid foundation of this kind. Moreover none of the parties regarded the work of the Assembly as final, for the monarchists looked forward to a future restoration of the throne, while their adversaries hoped to place the republic before long on a more secure and permanent footing. Hence the Assembly did no more than provide for the immediate organization of the government in as brief and practical a manner as possible. It passed three constitutional laws, as they are called, which are in the form of ordinary statutes, and very

may be found in Bozérian's *Etude sur la Révision de la Constitution,* and in Professor Currier's *Constitutional and Organic Laws of France.* The latter, published as a supplement to the *Annals of the American Academy of Political Science* (March, 1893), gives a translation into English of all these laws. See also an article by Saleilles on the "Development of the Present Constitution of France." (*Ann. Amer. Acad. of Pol. Sci.,* July, 1895.)

[1] Lebon, *Frankreich* (in Marquardsen's *Handbuch des Oeffentlichen Rechts*), p. 19.

short and concise. One of them, that of February 25, 1875, provides for the organization of the powers of the state. Another, that of February 24, 1875, deals in greater detail with the organization of the Senate. And the third, dated July 16, 1875, fixes the relations of the powers of the state among themselves.

The provisional character of the constitution is clearly

Amend-   seen in the method of amendment. It has
ments.
          been the habit in France to make a sharp distinction between the constituent and legislative powers, the former being withdrawn to a greater or less extent from the control of the Parliament. But in this instance both of the great parties wanted to facilitate changes in the fundamental laws, in order to be able to carry out their own plans whenever a favorable occasion might present itself.[1] A departure from tradition was therefore made, and it was provided that the constitutional laws could be amended by a National Assembly, or Congress, composed of the two branches of Parliament sitting together, which should meet for this purpose whenever both chambers on their own motion, or on that of the President of the Republic, declared the need of revision.[2] The constitutional laws have been

[1] Cf. Borgeaud, *Etablissement et Révision des Constitutions*, pt. iii. liv. ii. ch. viii.

[2] Const. Law of Feb. 25, 1875, Art. 8. It is not provided whether the Chambers shall declare in general terms that there is a need of revision, or whether they shall specify the revision to be made, and this point has given rise to lively debates; but on the two occasions when a revision was actually undertaken, the Chambers passed identical resolutions specifying the articles to be amended. (Lebon, *Frankreich*, pp. 74, 75 ; Saleilles, *op. cit.* pp. 6, 7, 9.)

twice amended in this way. On the first occasion (June 21, 1879), the provision making Versailles the capital was repealed, and thereupon a statute was passed transferring the seat of government to Paris.[1] On the second occasion (August 14, 1884), several amendments were made. Among these one of the most notable changed the provisions relating to the mode of electing senators, and another declared that the republican form of government cannot be made the subject of proposal for revision, — the object of the latter being to prevent the destruction of the Republic by constitutional means. The device of providing that a law shall never be repealed is an old one, but I am not aware that it has ever been of any avail.

This method of amendment has virtually rendered the Parliament omnipotent, for excepting the provision about changing the republican form of government, there is no restriction on its authority. The Chambers cannot, it is true, pass an amendment to the constitutional laws in the form of an ordinary statute, but if they are agreed they can pass it by meeting as a National Assembly. The power of the Chambers is therefore nearly as absolute as that of the British Parliament.[2] The principle, moreover, that the fundamental law cannot be changed by ordinary statute is devoid of legal sanction, for if the Chambers should choose to pass an act of this kind, no court or official could legally prevent its application.[3] But while the

[1] Law of July 22, 1879. This act provides, however, that the National Assembly shall meet at Versailles.

[2] Cf. Saleilles, *op. cit.*, p. 11.

[3] Cf. Laferrière, *Traite de la Jurisdiction Administrative*, vol. ii. p. 5.

constitution imposes no legal restraint on the Parliament, it would be a great mistake to suppose that it had no effect. On the contrary, it has such moral force that any attempt to pass a statute that clearly violated its terms would awake a strong repugnance; and indeed a suggestion by the president of one or other of the Chambers that a bill would be unconstitutional has more than once sufficed to prevent its introduction.[1] On the other hand, the fact that formal amendments can be made only in joint session, and only after both Chambers have resolved that there is a need of revision, has some influence in preventing changes in the text of the constitutional laws, because the Senate, being the more conservative body, and only half as large as the other House, is timid about going into joint session, not knowing what radical amendments may be proposed there, and fearing to be swamped by the votes of the deputies.

Let us now examine the organs of the state in succession, taking up first the Parliament with its two branches, the Senate and the Chamber of Deputies; then turning to the President as the chief magistrate of the Republic, and finally passing to the ministers as the connecting link between the Parliament and the President, and the controlling factor in the machinery of the state.

The composition of the Chamber of Deputies is left to ordinary legislation, except that the constitu-
The Chamber of Deputies. tional law of February 25, 1875, Art. 1, provides for its election by universal suffrage. By

---

[1] Lebon, *Frankreich*, p. 23.

statute the ballot is secret, and the franchise extends to
all men over twenty-one years of age who have not been
deprived of the right to vote in consequence of a conviction for crime, and who are not bankrupts, under
guardianship, or in active military or naval service.[1] To
be eligible a candidate must be twenty-five years old
and not disqualified from being a voter.[2] Members of
families that have ever reigned in France are, however,
excluded;[3] and in order to prevent as far as possible
the use of pressure the law forbids almost every state
official to be a candidate in a district where his position
might enable him to influence the election.[4] As a further safeguard against the power of the administration,
which is justly dreaded by the French Liberals, it is
provided that all public servants who receive salaries,
except a few of the highest in rank, shall lose their
offices if they accept an election to Parliament, and that
a deputy who is appointed even to one of these highest
offices, unless it be that of minister or under-secretary,
shall lose his seat.[5]

The Chamber of Deputies is elected for four years,
and consists at present of five hundred and
ninety-seven members; ten of the seats being
distributed among the various colonies, and six allotted
to Algiers, while the remaining deputies are chosen in

The method
of election.

[1] Arts. 1, 2, and 5 of the Law of Nov. 30, 1875. Poudra et Pierre,
Droit Parlementaire, sects. 482–84, 498–514.

[2] Law of Nov. 30, 1875, Arts. 6, 7.

[3] Law of June 16, 1885, Art. 4.

[4] Law of Nov. 30, 1875, Art. 12.

[5] *Id.*, Arts. 8, 9, and 11. A deputy appointed to one of these offices
may, however, be reëlected (Art. 11).

France. The method of election has varied from time to time between that of single electoral dis-

Scrutin de liste and *scrutin d'arron-dissement.*

tricts, a system called the *scrutin d'arron-dissement*, and that of the *scrutin de liste*, which consists in the choice of all the deputies from each department on a general ticket, the difference being the same that exists between our method of electing congressmen each in a separate district, and our method of choosing presidential electors on a single ticket for the whole State. The *scrutin d'arrondissement* or single district system prevailed from 1876 to 1885, when the *scrutin de liste* was revived;[1] partly, no doubt, in order to swamp the reactionary minority, but also with the hope of withdrawing the deputies from the pressure of petty local interests, which had become lamentably strong, of getting a Chamber of broader and more national views, and of forming a Republican majority that would be more truly a great and united party. The experiment did not last long enough to produce any sensible effect of this kind; and indeed the change seems, on the whole, to have resulted in an increase of the power of the local politicians, who formed themselves into nominating and electoral committees for the department. At the general elections of 1885 the Reactionaries gained rather than lost seats in spite of the *scrutin de liste;* and the disgust of the Republicans with the device from which they had hoped so much was brought to its height two or three years later, by General Boulanger. This singular man, who, after enjoying a marvelous popularity, became in a short time an object of

[1] Law of June 16, 1885.

contempt, if not of ridicule, had been minister of war in one of the recent Republican cabinets. He was forced to resign on account of his enormous expenditure on the army, and the fear that he would plunge the nation into a war with Germany. He then posed as the saviour of the country, and being at the height of his reputation he made use of the *scrutin de liste* to hold a *plébiscite* or popular vote of France piecemeal. Whenever a seat became vacant in a department he stood as a candidate, and if elected he held the seat only until a vacancy occurred in another department, when he resigned to appear as a candidate again. After doing this in several large departments he was able to declare that a considerable part of the French people had pronounced themselves on his side — a proceeding which would have been impossible if the deputies had been elected in five hundred and seventy-six separate districts. His success at the by-elections had so frightened the Republicans that they restored the *scrutin d'arrondissement* or single electoral districts before the general election of 1889 took place.[1]

Every large body of men, not under strict military discipline, has lurking in it the traits of a mob, and

---

[1] Law of Feb. 13, 1889. In order to frustrate more effectually Boulanger's scheme, a law of July 17, 1889, provided that no one should be candidate in more than one district. The meaning and effects of these laws is discussed by Saleilles (*Ann. Am. Acad. Pol. Sci.*, July, 1895, pp. 19–37). A measure providing for the restoration of the *scrutin de liste* with an arrangement for proportional representation passed the Chamber of Deputies in 1912. For the arguments in its favor, see "Electoral Reform in France," by J. W. Garner, *American Political Science Review*, vii, pp. 610–38 (Nov., 1913).

is liable to occasional outbreaks when the spirit of disorder becomes epidemic; but the French
Chamber of Deputies is especially tumultuous,
and, in times of great excitement, sometimes
breaks into a veritable uproar. Even the method of
preserving order lacks the decorum and dignity that
one expects in a legislative assembly. The President
has power to call a refractory member to order and
impose a penalty in case he persists; but instead of
relying on this alone, he often tries to enforce silence
by caustic remarks. The writer remembers being in
the Chamber a few years ago when M. Floquet was
presiding, — the same man who fought a duel with
General Boulanger and wounded him in the throat.
A deputy who had just been speaking kept interrupt-
ing the member who was addressing the Chamber, and
when called to order made some remark about parliamentary practice. The President cried out, "It is not
according to parliamentary practice for one man to
speak all the time." "I am not speaking all the time,"
said the deputy. "At this moment you are overbear-
ing everybody," answered the President. This incident
is related, not as being unusual or humorous, but as
a fair sample of what is constantly occurring in the
Chamber. Even real sarcasm does not seem to be
thought improper. Thus in a recent debate a deputy,
in the midst of an unusually long speech, was continually interrupted, when the President, Floquet, exclaimed, "Pray be silent, gentlemen. The member
who is speaking has never before approached so near
to the question."[1] These sallies from the chair are an

The Chamber a tumultuous body.

[1] *Journal Officiel* of Nov. 18, 1892.

old tradition in France, although, of course, their use depends on the personal character of the President. One does not, for example, find them at all in the reports of debates during the time Casimir-Perier was presiding over the Chamber. When the confusion gets beyond all control, and the President is at his wits' end, he puts on his hat, and if this does not quell the disturbance, he suspends the sitting for an hour in order to give time for the excitement to subside.

The French Senate consists of three hundred members, and by the constitutional law of February 24, 1875, two hundred and twenty-five of these were to be elected for nine years by the departments, while seventy-five were appointed for life by the same National Assembly that framed that law. The life senators were intended to be a permanent feature of the Senate, and it was provided that when any of them died his successor should be elected for life by the Senate itself. A few years later, however, the Republicans, thinking such an institution inconsistent with democracy, passed the amendment to the constitutional laws, to which a reference has already been made.[1] This, while leaving untouched the provisions relating to the existence and powers of the Senate, took away the constitutional character from those regulating the election of senators, which thus became subject to change by ordinary legislation. A statute was then passed (December 9, 1884) providing that as fast as the life senators died their seats should be distributed among the departments, so that nowadays all the senators

The Senate.

---

[1] Const. Law of Aug. 14, 1884.

alike are elected in the same way. There are eighty-six departments in France, and the senators are apportioned by the act among them according to population. Since the abolition of life senatorships, the number of seats belonging to a department varies from two up to ten, while the territory of Belfort, each of the three departments of Algiers, and several of the colonies are represented by one senator apiece.[1] The senators so elected hold office for nine years, one third retiring every three years.[2] They are chosen in each department of France by an electoral college composed of the deputies, of the members of the general council, of the members of the councils of the arrondissements, and of delegates chosen by the municipal councils of the communes of towns.[3] Before 1884 each commune elected only one delegate,[4] but by the law of that year the number of delegates increases with the size of the communes, though much less than in proportion to the population. These communal delegates form a large majority of the electoral college, and hence the Senate was called by Gambetta the Great Council of the Communes of France.[5]

A senator must be forty years old; and since the law of 1884 the disqualifications for this office have been the same as for that of member of the Chamber of Deputies.[6]

---

[1] Law of Dec. 9, 1884, Art. 2.

[2] *Id.*, Art. 7.

[3] *Id.*, Art. 6.

[4] Const. Law of Feb. 24, 1875, Art. 4.

[5] Saleilles, *op. cit.*, p. 41.

[6] Law of Dec. 9, 1884, Arts. 4, 5, and *Provisions Temporaires.* Law of Dec. 26, 1887. Lebon, *Frankreich*, pp. 63, 64, 67.

The legislative power of the Senate and the Chamber of Deputies is the same, except that financial Its func-
bills must originate in the latter;[1] but while tions.
it is admitted that the Senate may reduce proposals for taxes and appropriations, there is a dispute whether it can increase them or not, and debates on this point are constantly recurring. In practice the Chamber has sometimes accepted augmentations thus introduced, but more frequently the Senate has abandoned them.[2] The Senate has two peculiar functions. First, its consent is necessary for a dissolution of the Chamber of Deputies,[3] a provision designed as a safeguard against the President, who might otherwise dissolve the Chamber in order to attempt a *coup d'état* during its absence; and, second, the President is authorized, with the approval of the Council of Ministers, to constitute the Senate a high court to try any one for an attempt on the safety of the state.[4] This power was used in the case of General Boulanger, who failed to appear for trial, and was condemned in his absence.

With such an organization and powers, an American might suppose that the Senate would be a Its actual
more influential body than the Chamber of influence.

[1] Const. Law of Feb. 24, 1875, Art. 8.
[2] Dupriez, vol. ii. pp. 430–32.
[3] Const. Law of Feb. 25, 1875, Art. 5.
[4] Lebon, *Frankreich*, p. 73, Const. Laws of Feb. 24, 1875, Art. 9, and July 16, 1875, Art. 12. The procedure was regulated by a law of Aug. 10, 1889. By the Const. Law of July 16, 1875, Art. 12, the Chamber of Deputies can impeach the ministers, and in case of high treason the President of the Republic. The impeachments are tried by the Senate. For the interpretation put upon this clause, see Lebon, *Frankreich* pp. 55–58.

Deputies; but in reality it is by far the weaker body of the two, although it contains at least as much political ability and experience as the other House, and, indeed, has as much dignity, and is composed of as impressive a body of men as can be found in any legislative chamber the world over. The fact is that according to the traditions of the parliamentary system the cabinet is responsible only to the more popular branch of the legislature, and in all but one of the instances where a cabinet in France has resigned on an adverse vote of the Senate, the vote was rather an excuse for the withdrawal of a discredited ministry than the cause of its resignation.[1] The remaining case, which occurred during the year 1896, is the only one where the responsibility of the ministers to the Senate was fairly raised, and where anything like a real contest took place between the chambers. On this occasion the Senate did certainly force a united and vigorous cabinet to resign, but it was enabled to do so only because the

---

[1] Dupriez (vol. ii. pp. 453–54) mentions two such cases. One in 1876, when the cabinet, disliking a bill for an amnesty passed by the Chamber of Deputies, proposed in the Senate a compromise, which the latter, averse to any amnesty, rejected. The ministers thereupon resigned, but they had really been beaten in the Chamber of Deputies, and their only hope of restoring their prestige lay in forcing through the compromise. The other case was in 1890, when the Senate by a vote condemning the economic policy of the government, brought about a cabinet crisis. But the ministry was already divided within itself, and had almost broken in pieces a few days before. There appears to have been a third instance of the same kind in 1883. In that case the Fallières ministry resigned because the Senate rejected a bill on the expulsion of members of families that had reigned in France, but here again the cabinet was disunited and in a feeble condition before the vote in the Senate took place. (*Journal Officiel*, Feb. 18 and 19, 1883.)

majority in the Chamber of Deputies was highly precarious, for there can be no doubt that if the cabinet could have relied on the hearty support of the Chamber it would have defied the Senate as it had already done two months before.[1] It has been only in very excep-

[1] The history of this case may be summarized as follows : The Chamber of Deputies when elected contained a decided majority of Conservative Republicans, and for two years the successive cabinets represented their views, but by degrees the party became disintegrated, and in October, 1895, a Radical cabinet was formed, which succeeded in obtaining the support of a majority. Early in the new year the Minister of Justice, not being satisfied that the *Juge d'Instruction*, who was holding the inquest on the southern railroad frauds, was sufficiently zealous in discovering the offenders, took the case out of his hands and intrusted it to another magistrate. On February 11, the Senate, which was strongly conservative, passed a vote censuring this act as an interference with the course of justice. Two days later, the Chamber of Deputies expressed its confidence in the government ; whereupon the Senate, on February 15, repeated its former vote. On the 20th, the matter was again brought up in the Chamber of Deputies, and M. Bourgeois, the head of the cabinet, declared that he should not resign so long as he was upheld by the Chamber, which proceeded to reaffirm its vote of the week before. A number of the senators who had been opposed to the cabinet, finding that it would not yield, read in the Senate next day a declaration protesting against the refusal of the ministers to hold themselves responsible to the Senate as a violation of the Constitution, but saying that while as senators they reserved their constitutional right, they did not wish to suspend the legislative life of the country. The Senate thereupon adopted an order of the day approving this declaration, and thus virtually gave up for a time the attempt to make the ministers responsible to itself. (*Journal Officiel*, Feb. 12, 14, 16, 21, and 22, 1896.)

A little later the cabinet brought forward a bill for a progressive income tax, and succeeded on March 26 in getting the Chamber to adopt an order of the day approving of the general principal involved. The order, however, which was somewhat equivocal, was only carried by sixteen votes, and more than half of the deputies were believed to be opposed in their hearts to the tax. The Senate thought its opportunity had come, and again passed a vote of lack of confidence in the ministry, this time on the subject of foreign affairs. (*Journal Officiel*, April 4.) The result

tional cases, that the Upper House has upset the ministry. Moreover the question at issue in the struggle of 1896 was not whether the cabinet is responsible to the Senate to the same extent that it is to the Chamber, but simply whether the Senate can insist on the removal of a ministry to which it is peculiarly hostile. No one has ever doubted that under ordinary circumstances the ministers are responsible only to the Chamber. The majority in that body alone is considered in the formation of a cabinet, and an unfavorable vote there on any current matter of importance is followed by a change of ministers, while a similar vote in the Senate is not regarded as a reason for resignation.[1]

was no better than before, but the Senate felt the strength of its position, and was not to be ignored. On April 21, therefore, it took a bolder step by a resolution to postpone the vote on the credits asked for Madagascar "until it had before it a constitutional ministry having the confidence of the two Chambers." Instead of trying to continue the fight Bourgeois resigned, declaring to the Chamber of Deputies that as the representative of universal suffrage it ought to be supreme, but that, owing to the impossibility of insuring proper military service in Madagascar after the vote of the Senate, patriotism obliged him to withdraw. The Radicals in the Chamber succeeded in carrying a vote affirming once more the preponderance of the elect of universal suffrage, and urging the need of democratic reforms ; but a few days later a purely Conservative cabinet presented itself to the Chamber, and obtained a vote of confidence by a majority of forty-three. (*Journal Officiel*, April 22, 24, and May 1.)

The outcome of the affair justified the belief that the Chamber would not engage in a prolonged struggle to support the cabinet ; that while unwilling to turn the ministers out itself, it would not be sorry to have the Senate do so. Had the deputies been so thoroughly in earnest as to force a deadlock between the Chambers, the Senate could not have refused its consent to a dissolution, and would certainly have been obliged to give way if the elections had resulted in a victory for the cabinet.

[1] Since this was written the Briand ministry resigned on a vote in the Senate in March, 1913.

As a rule the Senate does not decide the fate of the ministries, and hence cannot control their policy. The result is that without sinking to the helplessness of the English House of Lords, it has become a body of secondary importance.[1] At one time it stood very low in public esteem, on account of its origin; for it was created by the Reactionaries in the National Assembly, and was regarded as a monarchical institution; and even after the greater part of its seats were occupied by Republicans, it was suspected of being only half-heartedly in favor of the republican form of government. Its condemnation of Boulanger increased its popularity by making it appear a real bulwark of the Republic against the would-be dictator; but the prejudice against it has by no means disappeared, and the extreme Radicals have never ceased to demand its abolition, although conservative feeling in France will doubtless remain strong enough to prevent such a step. How great the influence of the Senate will be in the future is not easy to foretell. Some people were of opinion that with life members gone, many of whom had been distinguished in letters, in science, or in war, it would lose a good deal of its prestige. To some extent this fear has been realized. But, on the other hand, men of mark are still elected, and now that the Senate is not afraid of being thought lukewarm or hostile to the Republic, and does not feel

---

[1] In his *Essays on Government* (chap. i) the writer has tried to prove that this must necessarily be the condition of one of two chambers wherever the cabinet is responsible to the other; and that the cabinet cannot in the long run be responsible to both.

its existence seriously threatened, it has acquired more
boldness and energy.[1] It is highly improbable, moreover, that it will become utterly powerless, so long as
the deputies are divided into a number of political
groups, and the ministers are not able to speak with
authority as the leaders of a great and united party.

Although the Senate has little or no share in directing
the policy of the cabinet, it must not be supposed that
it is a useless body. On the contrary, it does very valuable work in correcting the over-hasty legislation of the
other Chamber, and in case of disagreement often has
its own way or effects a compromise.[2]

The two Chambers meeting in joint session form

*The Na-
tional
Assembly.*
what is called the National Assembly, which,
as we have seen, has power to revise the constitutional laws. It has one other function,
that of electing the President of the Republic. This

*The Presi-
dent of the
Republic.*
officer is chosen for seven years, and is re-
eligible;[3] the only limit on the choice of a
candidate being found in the constitutional
law of August 14, 1884, which excludes all members
of families that have ever reigned in France, — a provision dictated by the fear that, like Napoleon III., a
prince might use the presidency as a step to the throne.
The President is at the head of the Republic, but he
lives and travels in a style that is almost regal, for the
conception of a republic as severe, simple, and econom-

[1] Dupriez, vol. ii. pp. 382–83. The present position and the probable
future of the Senate are discussed by Saleilles, *op. cit.*, pp. 37–52.

[2] Dupriez, vol. ii. pp. 413–15.

[3] Const. Law of Feb. 25, 1875, Art. 2.

ical has changed very much in France since the second Empire taught the nation extravagance.[1]

The duties of the President, like those of every chief magistrate, are manifold. He is the executive head of the nation, and as such executes the laws, issues ordinances,[2] and appoints all the officers of the government.[3] He has also certain functions of a legislative character, but, except for the right of initiative in legislation, these are not in fact very extensive. He has no veto upon the laws, and although he may require the Chambers to reconsider a bill, the right has never been exercised.[4] With the consent of the Senate he can dissolve the Chamber of Deputies,[5] but this power has also fallen into disuse, because the members of his cabinet are very much under the control of the deputies, who dread the risk and expense of an election; and, in fact, a dissolution has not taken place since President MacMahon's unsuccessful attempt to use it in 1877 as a means of getting a Chamber in sympathy with his views. The President has power to make treaties; but treaties of peace, of commerce, those which burden the finances, affect the persons or property of French citizens in foreign countries, or which change the territory of France (in other words, all the more im-

His functions.

[1] Cf. G. Channes, *Nos Fautes*, Letter of Jan., 1885; Theodore Stanton in the *Arena*, Oct., 1891.

[2] For the nature of this power, see pp. 42–44, *infra*.

[3] Const. Law of Feb. 25, 1875, Art. 3.

[4] Const. Law of July 16, 1875, Art. 7; Dupriez, vol. ii. p. 369. It is not likely to be used unless after the bill has passed the cabinet that favored it has resigned, and another hostile to it has come in.

[5] Const. Law of Feb. 25, 1875, Art. 5.

portant ones), require the ratification of the Chambers.[1] A declaration of war also requires their consent;[2] but as a matter of fact the government managed to wage war in Tunis and Tonquin without any such consent, alleging at first that the affair was not a war, and afterwards defending itself on the ground that the Parliament by voting credits had virtually sanctioned its course.[3]

Unlike the President of the United States, the French President is not free to use his powers accord-

His Powers are really exercised by the ministers in his name.

ing to his own judgment, for in order to make him independent of the fate of cabinets, and at the same time to prevent his personal power from becoming too great, the constitutional laws declare that he shall not be responsible for his official conduct, except in case of high treason, and that all his acts of every kind, to be valid, must be countersigned by one of the ministers; and thus, like the British monarch, he has been put under guardianship and can do no wrong.[4] When, therefore, we speak of the powers of the President, it must be remembered that these are really exercised by the ministers, who are responsible to the Chamber of Deputies. The President, indeed, is not usually present at the cabinet consultations (*conseils de cabinet*) in which the real policy of the government is discussed, and as a rule he presides only over the formal meetings (*conseils des mi-*

---

[1] Const. Law of July 16, 1875, Art. 8.

[2] *Id.*, Art. 9.

[3] See Lebon, *Frankreich*, pp. 46, 47.

[4] Const. Law of Feb. 25, 1875, Arts. 3 and 6.

nistres) held for certain purposes specified by law.[1] He has power, it is true, to select the ministers, and in this matter he can use his own discretion to some extent, but in fact he generally intrusts some one with the formation of a cabinet, and appoints the ministers this man suggests.[2] His duty in these cases is not, however, as simple as that of the English King, because, for reasons that will be discussed in the next chapter, there is usually on the fall of a cabinet no leader of a victorious opposition to whom he can turn. A good deal of tact and skill is sometimes required at cabinet crises, and it is said that on one occasion the formation of a ministry was due to the personal influence of President Carnot.[3]

Sir Henry Maine makes merry over the exalted office and lack of power of the President. "There is," he says, "no living functionary who occupies a more pitiable position than a French President. The old kings of France reigned and governed. The Constitutional King, according to M. Thiers, reigns, but does not govern. The President of the United States governs, but he does not reign. It has been reserved for the President of the French Republic neither to reign nor yet to govern."[4]

At first sight the situation does, indeed, appear somewhat irrational. When the head of the state is desig-

[1] Lebon, *Frankreich,* p. 53 ; Dupriez, vol. ii. pp. 350–51 and 367–68, states that the President is often present when important matters are discussed, but cannot influence the decision.

[2] Dupriez, vol. ii. p. 340.

[3] See "France under M. Constans," in *Murray's Magazine* for May, 1890.

[4] *Popular Government,* p. 250.

nated by the accident of birth it is not unnatural to make of him an idol, and appoint a high priest to speak in his name; but when he is carefully selected as the man most fit for the place, it seems a trifle illogical to intrust the duties of the office to some one else. By the constitution of Sieyès an ornamental post of a similar character was prepared for the First Consul, but Napoleon said he had no mind to play the part of a pig kept to fatten. In government, however, the most logical system is not always the best, and the anomalous position of the President has saved France from the danger of his trying to make himself a dictator, while the fact that he is independent of the changing moods of the Chambers has given to the Republic a dignity and stability it had never enjoyed before. It is a curious commentary on the nature of human ambition, that in spite of the small power actually wielded by the President in France, the presidential fever seems to have nearly as strong a hold on public men as in this country.

Before proceeding to consider the ministers, there is one other institution which claims attention on account of its past rather than its present position. This is the *Conseil d'Etat* or Council of State,[1] a body whose importance has varied a great deal

The *Conseil d'Etat.*

---

[1] Aucoc, *Conférences sur le Droit Adm.*, liv. ii. ch. i. § 3; Ducrocq, *Cours de Droit Adm.*, tit. i. ch. i. sec. i. § iii.; Bœuf, *Résumé sur le Droit Adm.*, ed. of 1895, p. 32 et seq.; cf. Lebon, *Frankreich*, pp. 96–98; Dupriez, vol. ii. pp. 285–316, *passim*, and pp. 481–92; Goodnow, *Comparative Administrative Law*, vol. i. pp. 107–13. See also articles entitled "Le Conseil d'Etat et les Projets de Réforme," by Varagnac, *Revue des Deux Mondes*, Aug. 15 and Sept. 15, 1892.

at different times.   Under Napoleon I., and again dur‑
ing the second Empire, in addition to the possession of
executive functions, it was a real source of legislation ;
while at the time of the Restoration and the Monarchy
of July it became what it is to-day, a council with high
attributes, but very little authority.   Except as a court
of administrative justice,[1] it has now lost most of its
influence ; for although it must be consulted before
certain classes of ordinances can be issued, and may be
consulted on other administrative matters, its advice
need never be followed ; and in fact the habit of con‑
sulting it is said to have become little more than a mere
form.[2]   The legislative functions of the Council have
faded even more completely to a shadow, as is proved
by the fact that while the Government or either of the
Chambers may seek its aid in the framing of statutes,
the privilege is rarely exercised by the ministers, scarcely
at all by the Senate, and never by the Chamber of
Deputies.

The members of the Council are divided into several
classes, but those belonging to the most important class,
and the only ones who can vote when the Council sits
as a court, are appointed and dismissed at will by the
President of the Republic.[3]

[1] For its functions of this nature, see pp. 55–61, *infra*.

[2] "La Réforme Administrative — La Justice," by Vicomte d'Avenel,
Revue des Deux Mondes, June 1, 1889, pp. 597–98.

[3] The other members are also appointed by the President subject to
certain conditions, but as he can dismiss any of them, their tenure of office
depends on the pleasure of the cabinet, and in fact by means of resigna‑
tions or removals, most of the councilors were changed in 1879 in order
to make the council Republican. — "Le Conseil d'Etat," Varagnac,
Revue des Deux Mondes, Sept. 15, 1892, p. 295.

In a parliamentary system the ministers have two
The minis-   distinct functions. One of these is the same
ters.
as that of the members of the President's
Cabinet in the United States, and consists of the management of the departments of the administration.
The other is the duty of representing the government in
the Chambers, urging the adoption of its measures, and
defending its policy against the attacks of its adversaries. These two functions are not necessarily united,
and in fact it has been a common habit in some countries to appoint ministers without portfolios, as it is
called, that is, without any executive duties at all, in
order that they may devote their whole energy to the
battles in Parliament.[1] Although there is nothing to
prevent such a practice in France, it is not followed
to-day, each minister being at the head of a particular
branch of the administration. The number of departments, however, and the distribution of the public business among them is not fixed by law, but is regulated
from time to time by decree of the President of the
Republic. The number of ministers is, therefore, constantly liable to change according to the immediate
needs of the public service. At present there are twelve
departments or ministries : those of the Interior ; of
Justice ; of Foreign Affairs ; of Finance ; of War ; of
the Navy ; of Education and the Fine Arts ; of Public Works ; of Labor ; of Commerce, Industry, and

---

[1] This practice virtually exists in England, because some of the offices
held by the ministers, such as that of First Lord of the Treasury, and
that of Chancellor of the Duchy of Lancaster, involve no administrative
duties.

Posts and Telegraphs; of Agriculture; and of the Colonies.[1]

The constitutional law of February 25, 1875 (Art. 6), declares that the ministers are collectively responsible to the Chambers for the general policy of the government, and individually for their personal acts. Their responsibility to the Chambers. The object of this clause was, of course, to establish the parliamentary system, and in fact the French ministry is responsible to the Chamber of Deputies, as the English is to the House of Commons, and resigns on a hostile vote on any matter of importance. Except, indeed, for the Ministers of War and of the Navy, who are usually military men, the cabinet officers are almost always selected from among the members of Parliament,[2] although the reason for this practice in England does not apply in France, because the ministers have a right to be present and speak in either Chamber, whether members of it or not.[3]

But in order to understand fully the position of the French ministers, and their relation to the Parliament, it is necessary to realize their enormous power, and this is due largely to Their enormous power and its causes. three causes, — the paternal nature of the government, the centralization of the state, and the possession by the executive of authority that in an Anglo-Saxon

[1] Bœuf, *Résumé*, ed. of 1895, pp. 22, 23. The last ministry, that of the Colonies, was, however, created by statute in 1894, and as Bœuf remarks, the Chambers can always prevent the creation of a ministry by refusing to make the necessary appropriations.

[2] Dupriez, vol. ii. p. 336.

[3] Const. Law of July 16, 1875, Art. 6. In practice this privilege is also accorded to their under-secretaries. Lebon, *Frankreich*, p. 52.

country would be lodged with the legislature or the courts of law.

On the first of these matters, the paternal nature of

Paternal nature of the government.

the government, there is no need to dwell at length. All governments are growing more paternal at the present day, for a reaction has set in against the extreme *laissez-faire* doctrines preached by Adam Smith, John Stuart Mill, and the English political economists of the earlier school. There is a general tendency to restrain the liberty of the individual and subject him to governmental supervision and control. Such control and supervision are traditional in France, and far exceed anything to which we are accustomed in this country. All trades and occupations are there subject to a great deal more police inspection than with us. They require more generally to be licensed, and are regulated and prohibited by the administrative officials with a much freer hand. And although the liberty of the press and the right of holding public meetings are now substantially realized, the right of association is still very limited, for no society of more than twenty persons, except business companies, and associations of persons pursuing the same profession or trade, can be formed without the permission of the Minister of the Interior or the prefect of the department.[1] It is easy to see how much power all this paternalism places in the hands of the administration.

An explanation of the centralization of the state entails a brief survey of local government; and here

---

[1] Lebon, *Frankreich*, pp. 32–39 ; Ducrocq, tit. ii. ch. iii. ; ch. iv. sec. iii.

we meet with a deeply rooted French tradition, for centralization was already great under the old régime, and although the first effect of the Revolution was to place the administration of local affairs under the control of independent elected bodies, the pressure of foreign war, and the necessity of maintaining order at home, soon threw despotic power into the hands of the national government. Under Napoleon this power became crystallized in a permanent form, and an administrative system was established, more perfect, more effective, and at the same time more centralized than that which had existed under the monarchy.[1] The outward form of the Napoleonic system has been continuously preserved with surprisingly little change, but since 1830 its spirit has been modified in two distinct ways: first, by means of what the French call deconcentration, that is, by giving to the local agents of the central government a greater right of independent action, so that they are more free from the direct tutelage of the ministers; second, by a process of true decentralization, or the introduction of the elective principle into local government, and the extension of the powers of the local representative bodies. But although the successive rulers of France have pursued this policy pretty steadily, the progress of local self-government has been far from rapid.[2] One reason for

Centralization.

---

[1] For a short but vigorous comment on Napoleon's system, see G. L. Dickinson, *Revolution and Reaction in Modern France*, ch. ii.

[2] On the subject of local government, I have used Aucoc, *Conférences*, 3d ed. ; Bœuf, *Résumé*, ed. of 1895 ; Leroy-Beaulieu, *Adm. Locale en France et en Angleterre ;* Lebon's two works on France ; Goodnow, *Comp. Adm. Law.* There is a popular account in Block, *Entretiens familiers sur l'Adm. de notre pays.*

this is the habit of looking to the central authorities for guidance in all matters. Another is a fear on the part of the government of furnishing its enemies with rallying-points which might be used to organize an opposition, — a fear that takes shape to-day in provisions forbidding the local elected councils to express any opinions on general politics, or to communicate with each other except about certain matters specified by law. A third cause of the feeble state of local self-government is to be found in the fact that the Revolution of 1789 destroyed all the existing local divisions except the commune, and replaced them by artificial districts which have never developed any real vitality, so that the commune is the only true centre of local life in the republic.[1] A fourth, and perhaps the most potent cause of all, is the dread of disorder which is constantly present in the minds of Frenchmen, and makes them crave a master strong enough to cope with any outbreak.

France is divided into eighty-six departments, at the

Local government. — The department and the prefect. head of each of which is a prefect, appointed and removed at pleasure by the President of the Republic, but in reality nominated by the Minister of the Interior. The office is, indeed, regarded as distinctly political, and the incumbent is often replaced when the minister changes. The prefect, who is by far the most important of the local officials, occupies a double position, for he is the agent of the central government in regard to those matters of general administration which are thought to concern

---

[1] Most of the existing communes were in fact created in 1789.

the whole country, and at the same time he is the executive officer of the department for local affairs. In the former capacity he is in theory the immediate subordinate of the Minister of the Interior, but since his duties extend to all branches of the administration, he corresponds in practice directly with any minister in whose sphere of action the matter with which he is called upon to deal may lie. His authority as the agent of the central government is not, however, the same in all cases. Sometimes he is absolutely subject to the orders of the ministers. This is true when he executes general laws and ordinances; but when, for example, he directs the police of the department, or supervises the subordinate local bodies, he proceeds on his own responsibility, and his acts can be overruled by the central government only in case they are contrary to law, or give rise to complaints on the part of the persons affected by them. In pursuance of the policy of deconcentration, the prefect has been given an independent authority of this kind over a large number of subjects, and he was intended to exercise his own judgment in regard to them, but the influence and pressure of the deputies has, it is said, induced him to shirk responsibility as much as possible by referring doubtful questions to the ministers, and hence the centralization has not been diminished as much as was expected.[1] In matters of general administration, the prefect is assisted by a prefectoral council of three or four members appointed by the President of the Republic; but, except when it sits as an administrative

[1] Channes, Letter of October 1, 1884.

court, the functions of this body are almost altogether advisory, and their use has become scarcely more than a form.[1]

As the executive officer for local affairs, the prefect carries out the resolutions of the General Council. This is the representative assembly of the department, and is elected by universal suffrage, one of the members being chosen in each canton for six years, and half of them being renewed every three years. The authority of the body is jealously limited. Its competence is almost entirely confined to affairs that are deemed to have a strictly local interest,[2] and even in regard to these its powers are not absolute, for its votes on certain matters can be annulled by the President of the Republic, and its budget, that is the annual tax levy and list of appropriations, is not valid without his approval. Although the Council has the right of final decision in a considerable class of subjects, its actual power over them is curtailed in a variety of ways. In the first place it does not carry out its own votes, but their execution is intrusted to an agent of the central government, the prefect, who appoints all the officials, manages the public institutions, and signs the orders for all payments of money; the direct control of the council over his performance of these duties extending only to the election of a standing commission which has little more than a right of inspec-

The General Council.

[1] Vicomte d'Avenel, "La Réforme Administrative," *Revue des Deux Mondes*, June 1, 1889, p. 596.

[2] Its functions in relation to the general administration consist in apportioning certain direct taxes, in giving its advice when asked, and in expressing its wishes on matters not connected with general politics.

tion.[1]   In the second place, the prefect has an opportunity to exert a great deal of influence over the action
of the Council, for not only has he a right to address
it, but he prepares the budget and all other business,
and in fact it is not allowed to act on any matter until
it has heard his report.[2]   Moreover the Council is only
permitted to sit a very short time.   It has two regular
sessions a year, whose duration is limited one to a
month, the other to a fortnight, and although extra
sessions can be held they must not exceed one week
apiece.   Finally its very existence is insecure, for it can
be dissolved by the chief of the state.   In general it
may be said that in matters falling within its province
the General Council cannot do everything it wants, but
can prevent almost anything it does not want.   Its
financial resources are not large,[3] and its attention is
confined for the most part to the construction of roads,
subventions to railroads, and the care of schools, insane
asylums, and other institutions of a similar character.

At one time a hope was entertained that politics
might be kept out of the general councils, but it has
not been fulfilled, the departmental elections being
regularly conducted on party lines.[4]   It has therefore

[1] The Council can delegate to the commission a somewhat indefinite
class of functions, but it is not in fact a body of much importance.   Dupriez, vol. ii. pp. 467–68.

[2] Aucoc, p. 282.

[3] Almost its only source of revenue is the addition of a limited sum to
the direct state taxes.

[4] Bozérian, in his *Etude sur la Révision de la Constitution* (pp. 89–90),
attributes this to the fact that the local assemblies take part in the election of senators.

been thought best to intrust the supervision of the
communes largely to the central government and its
representative the prefect, rather than to the councils
with their partisan bias, and this, of course, deprives
the latter of a part of the importance they would otherwise possess.[1]

The next local division is the arrondissement. This
is a mere administrative district without corporate personality, with no property, revenues,
or expenses of its own, and although it has a sub-prefect and an elected council, neither of them has much
power. In fact it has been proposed to abolish the
arrondissement altogether.

The arron-
dissement.

The canton, which is the next subdivision, is really a
judicial and military rather than an administrative district, and therefore does not concern us here.

The can-
ton.

We now come to the communes, which are the smallest local entities, but differ enormously in
area and population. They vary in size from
twenty acres to over a quarter of a million, and they
run all the way from a hamlet with a dozen inhabitants
to large cities; yet with the exception of Paris and
Lyons they are all governed on one plan. The officer
in the commune whose position corresponds
to that of the prefect in the department is
the mayor. He acts in the same way both as agent of
the central government, and as the executive head of the

The com-
mune.

The mayor.

---

[1] By the law of 1884 on municipalities, part of the supervision over these
bodies, which had previously been in the hands of the general councils,
was withdrawn and given to the prefect.

district, but whereas in the prefect the former character predominates, the mayor is chiefly occupied with local matters. It is largely for this reason that, unlike the prefect, he is not appointed by the President, but since 1884 has been elected by and from the communal council for the length of its own term.[1] The mayor is, however, by no means free from control. So far as he acts as agent of the central government, he is absolutely under the orders of the prefect. Nor is this all. The subject of communal police, which includes the public health and other matters of a kindred nature, is considered a part of the local administration, but the acts of the mayor in regard to it can be annulled by the prefect, who has also power in many cases to issue direct orders of his own. Moreover the police officials require to be confirmed by the prefect,[2] and can be removed only by him.[3] But even these extensive powers of control are not deemed enough, and it is provided that the mayor can be suspended from office for a month by the prefect, or for three months by the Minister of the Interior, and can be removed altogether by the President of the Republic.

The deliberative organ of the commune is the communal council, which varies in size from ten to thirty-six members, and is elected by universal suffrage for four years. Its authority extends to all communal

[1] The office is an honorary one, as the mayor receives no salary.

[2] Or sub-prefect.

[3] The mayor is not free from control in regard to other matters of local interest, for his accounts must be submitted for approval to the prefect, who can order the payment of any expense properly authorized if the mayor neglects to make it.

affairs, except that it has nothing to do with the broad
subject of police, although that is regarded for other
purposes as a local matter. The general statute on
municipal government lays down the general principle that the decisions of the council on local affairs,
when legally made, are conclusive without the approval
of any superior administrative official, but in a subsequent section all the most important matters are specially excepted from the rule. The list of exceptions
includes almost every financial measure, the construction
of roads and buildings, and the sale of communal property.[1] The council has, therefore, very much less power
than might at first sight be supposed; and in order to
guard against any attempt on its part to exceed these
slender privileges, the prefect is given a discretionary
authority to suspend it for a month, while the President
of the Republic can dissolve it entirely, and appoint a
commission with limited powers to rule the commune
for two months, when a new election must take place.

The general laws of local government already de-
scribed do not, however, cover the whole
field, because a dread of the explosive character and communistic tendencies of the democracy of
Paris has prevented the capital from enjoying even the
measure of liberty granted to other towns. The city
has, indeed, a municipal council composed of eighty
elected members and endowed with most of the usual
powers, and a general council for the department with
limited powers, composed of these same eighty rein-

Paris.

---

[1] The official who has power to approve the budget can also inscribe
therein certain obligatory expenses.

forced by eight suburban members; but the executive authority is entirely in the hands of the central government. It is lodged in part with the mayors of the twenty arrondissements, who are appointed directly by the President of the Republic; but chiefly with two prefects appointed in the same way. One of these, the Prefect of the Seine, has most of the functions of the ordinary prefect, together with those of a central mayor; while the other, the Prefect of Police, has charge of the police, and is directly responsible to the Minister of the Interior.[1]

This sketch of local government in France shows how centralized the state still remains, what extensive supervision and control the administration keeps in its own hands, and how slight is the measure of real local autonomy if measured by an Anglo-Saxon standard. In fact, the central government still makes itself continually and actively felt in local affairs, and this is for the ministers a great source of power, but also, as we shall see later, a cause of weakness.

A third source of the enormous power of the ministers in France is the possession by the executive of authority that in an Anglo-Saxon country would be lodged with the legislature or the courts of law. This requires an explanation, for it involves some of the most strange and

Legislative and judicial powers of the executive.

---

[1] In Lyons the control of the police is still intrusted to the Prefect of the Rhone; in Marseilles it is in charge of the Prefect of Bouches-du-Rhône. In all cities of over 40,000 people the organization of the police is fixed by decree of the chief of the state, although the members of the force are appointed as in other communes.

interesting peculiarities of French, and, indeed, of continental political ideas.

Let us take first the legislative authority of the executive in France. When an English or an American legislator drafts a statute he tries to cover all questions that can possibly arise. He goes into details and describes minutely the operation of the act, in order that every conceivable case may be expressly and distinctly provided for. He does this because there is no one who has power to remedy defects that may subsequently appear. If the law is vague or obscure, it can receive an authoritative interpretation only from the courts by the slow process of litigation. If it is incomplete, it must remain so until amended by a subsequent enactment. In some cases, it is true, an officer or board is given by statute power to make regulations. The Local Government Board and our boards of health furnish examples of this; but such cases are exceptional, and most Anglo-Saxons feel that the power is in its nature arbitrary, and ought not to be extended farther than is necessary. And here it is important to distinguish between rules issued by the head of a department for the guidance of his subordinates and the regulations of which we are speaking. The former are merely directions given to the officials for the purpose of instructing them in their duties, and are binding on no one else. The right to issue them must belong, to some extent, to every one who has other persons under his orders, although they are used much more systematically in France than in the United States. The regulations with which we are concerned here are

Legislative
decrees and
ordinances.

of quite a different kind, for they are binding on all
citizens who may be affected by them, and have, in fact,
the character of laws.

In America the authority to make regulations is de-
legated by the legislature cautiously, and apart from
such an express delegation no officer of the government has power to issue any ordinances with the force
of law. But in France all this is very different. Statutes that do not concern the rights of a man against
his neighbor, that do not, in other words, form a part
of the Civil Code, are often couched in general terms,
and enunciate a principle which the Executive is to
carry out in detail.[1] Sometimes the President of the
Republic is expressly given power to make regulations,
but even without any special authority he has a general
power to make them for the purpose of completing the
statutes, by virtue of his general duty to execute the
laws.[2] Such regulations in France are called acts of
secondary legislation, and the ordinances of the President in which they are contained are termed *décrets*.
The power to make them is not, however, confined to
the chief of the state. For matters of inferior gravity the laws often confer a similar authority on the ministers, the prefects, and even the mayors, and in this

[1] Dupriez (vol. ii. p. 377), after remarking this difference between
English and French legislation, expresses a regret that the French Parliament has shown a tendency of late years to go more into details.

[2] On the power to issue ordinances in France, see Aucoc, *Conférences*,
§§ 52–57, 66, 91, 170 ; Ducrocq, *Cours*, §§ 61–66, 72–73, 109–10, 210–14 ;
Goodnow, vol. i. pp. 85–87.

Before issuing certain classes of ordinances the President must consult
the Council of State, but he is not obliged to follow its advice.

case the edicts are termed *arrêtés*, to distinguish them from the more solemn ordinances of the President.[1] The regulations cannot, of course, be contrary to law, or in excess of the authority of the official who issues them. If they are so and infringe private rights, a process to have them annulled may be instituted before the administrative courts, and in certain limited cases the ordinary courts can also refuse to apply them.[2]

So much for the power of the executive to make law, Appropriations. but this does not exhaust its encroachments on what we have learned to regard as the province of the legislature, for it is less strictly held to the appropriations voted by the Chambers than is the case with us. The *virements* (that is to say, the use for one purpose of appropriations voted for another), which were an abuse under the Empire, have, indeed, been abolished, except as between different items in the same chapter of the annual budget; but certain chapters are designated each year to which additions can be made by decree of the President issued with the consent of the council of ministers. Moreover, in urgent and unforeseen cases arising when Parliament is not in session, the government has power by means of such a decree, not only to incur the expenses called for by the emergency, but also to open an extraordinary credit on its own authority and borrow the money that it needs.[3]

[1] Lebon, *Frankreich*, p. 23 ; Aucoc, Ducrocq, *ubi cit.*

[2] Laferrière, *Traité de la Jur. Adm.*, liv. iii. ch. i. sec. II. ; liv. vi. ; liv. vii. ch. i. sec. IV.

[3] In both cases notice of the decree must be laid before the Chambers within fourteen days from their next meeting. (Lebon, *Frankreich*, p. 162.) It is worth while, moreover, to note in passing that there is

One may, perhaps, be pardoned for dwelling at some- what greater length on the judicial powers of the executive in France, both because they are so little understood by English-speaking people, and because their origin may be traced to a tradition which has its roots far back in the past.

_{Judicial powers of the execu- tive.}

The characteristic difference between the political history of England and that of France is to be found in the fact that the English, though influenced by each new spirit of the age, have never yielded entirely to its guidance, while the French have always thrown themselves into the current, and, adopting completely the dominant ideas of the time, have carried them to their logical results. Thus, in the Middle Ages, the feudal system never became fully developed in England as it did in France. Again, when absolute monarchy came into vogue, the British sovereign was not able to acquire the arbitrary power of the Bourbons. And, lastly, democracy made its way neither so rapidly nor so thoroughly on the north as on the south of the Chan- nel. The result is that in France the institutions of any period have been adapted almost exclusively to the wants of the time in which they were produced, and in the succeeding age it has been thought necessary to destroy them and devise new ones more in harmony

_{Character- istic differ- ence between English and French his- tory.}

no effective process for bringing to account a minister who exceeds the appropriations. He can, indeed, be impeached, but except in times of great excitement this would not be done if the money had been expended for public purposes ; and as regards civil liability, there is no court that has power to compel him to refund the sums which he has spent illegally.

48 FRANCE.

with the new conditions;[1] whereas in England there
has been no need of such sweeping changes, and it has
been possible to preserve in a modified form many of
the most important features of the government. Hence
the permanence and continuity of the political system.[2]
Let us inquire how these facts have affected the development of judicial and administrative institutions in
the two countries.

The Norman kings of England strove deliberately to
check the growth of the feudal system, and
their successors constantly followed the same
policy. Now the essence of the feudal system consisted in the blending of public and
private law by making all political relations depend on
the tenure of land; and, in fact, according to the strict
feudal theory, no man had direct relations with any
superior except his immediate overlord. Every great
vassal of the crown, therefore, had jurisdiction over all
the tenants on his estate, which he exercised by holding
a court of his own for the administration of justice
among them. The English kings resisted this principle,
and tried to bring their power to bear directly on all
the people of the realm. For this purpose
sheriffs were appointed to represent the crown
in the counties, and what was of more permanent importance, the gravest crimes, actions for the possession

Early de-
velopment
of the royal
power in
England.

The judicial
system.

---

[1] This is the more striking because the French are in some ways more
conservative than the English, as, for example, in their retention to the
present day of public executions. M. Lebon truly remarks (*France as
It Is*, p. 86): "People have no idea of the spirit of routine and conser-
vatism which prevails in France."

[2] Cf. Freeman, *Growth of the English Constitution*, pp. 63–66.

of land, and subsequently other matters, were brought within the jurisdiction of the *Curia Regis*.[1] As early as the reign of Henry I., moreover, royal officers were commissioned to travel about the country holding court, a practice which was renewed in a more systematic form by Henry II., and has continued with short interruptions to the present day.[2] The chief object of the early kings in sending out the itinerant justices, as they were called, was no doubt financial; for their duties consisted in assessing taxes, collecting fines for violation of the law, and administering justice, which was in itself a source of no small profit in the Middle Ages.[3] The functions of the justices in the collection of revenue grew, however, less and less prominent, but their administration of justice became of permanent importance, and in regard to this two tendencies were at work. In the first place, the royal judges adopted new methods of procedure and gradually developed the trial by jury, while the baronial courts clung to the ordeal and other barbaric forms of trial.[4] "The gladsome light of jurisprudence," as Coke called it, came

[1] See Pollock & Maitland, *History of English Law*, vol. i. pp. 85–87 and chs. v. and vi.

[2] The institution of traveling judges was not new. It had been used by Charlemagne (Hallam, *Middle Ages*, ch. ii. part ii. 5), and a similar practice was employed by Alfred, Edgar, and Canute (Stubbs, *History of England*, xi. §§ 127, 134). On the itinerant justices, see Stubbs, *Ib.* xi. 127 ; xii. 141, 145, 150 ; xiii. 163 ; xv. 235 ; Gneist, *Englische Verfassungsgeschichte*, pp. 148, 224–28, 305 (note), 318–19, 447. Pollock & Maitland, vol. i. pp. 134, 149, 179 ; Franqueville, *Le Système Judiciaire de la Grande Bretagne*, vol. i. pp. 149 *et seq.* The royal duty of sending the justices in eyre is one of those insisted upon in Magna Charta, § 18.

[3] Stubbs, *Ib.* xi. 127.

[4] Cf. Stubbs, *Ib.* xiii. 164 ; Gneist, *Ib.* p. 142.

with the king's courts, and hence it is not surprising that they supplanted the baronial courts, and in time drew before themselves all the important lawsuits. In the second place, the commissions which had at first been issued to high officials, barons, and knights, became confined to regular judges, and about the time of Edward I. were given only to the members of the royal courts at Westminster.[1] The same body of judges, therefore, expounded the law in all parts of the realm, and hence England, alone among the countries of Europe, developed a uniform national justice called the common law.[2] The people naturally became attached to this law and boasted of the rights of Englishmen, while the courts that were the creators and guardians of the law became strong and respected.

The very fact that the judicial branch of the government became so highly developed made the centralization of the administration unnecessary. At the time when the itinerant justices first went on circuit, administration in the modern sense was of course unknown, and such local affairs as needed attention were regulated by the shire moots and other local meetings.[3] The sheriff, indeed, represented the crown, but his powers were curtailed more and more, until, apart from his command of the military forces of the county, he became little more than an officer of the courts.[4] When the local administra-

The administrative system.

---

[1] Gneist, *Englische Verfassungsgeschichte*, p. 318 ; Stubbs, *History of England*, xv. 235.

[2] Cf. Hallam, *Middle Ages*, ch. viii. part ii. 3.

[3] Stubbs, *Ib.* xv. 205.

[4] On the powers of the sheriff, see Stubbs, *Ib.* xiii. 163, xv. 204–7 ; Gneist, *Ib.* pp. 115–20, 297.

tion grew more important, it was confided not to him, but to justices of the peace, who, though nominally selected by the king, were never strictly under his orders, and in time became almost completely independent, except for the purely judicial control exercised by the Court of King's Bench.[1]

In England, therefore, the royal power came early into contact with the people all over the kingdom by means of the courts of law, and the judicial system became highly centralized; while the local administrative institutions developed slowly, and through them the king's authority was little felt. In France, on the other hand, the course of events was very different, for the royal power came into direct contact with the people at a much later date, and therefore in quite another form. When the feudal system became established, the great vassals set up their own courts and succeeded in excluding the royal judges from their fiefs, so that the direct jurisdiction of the crown became confined to the comparatively small part of the country which was included in the royal domain. Gradually, indeed, as the feudal system began to lose its strength, the king's jurisdiction encroached upon that of the vassals, — a process which was carried on both by insisting on the right of appeal to the royal tribunals, and by reserving for the exclusive cognizance of the king's courts a somewhat indefinite class of cases

Development of the direct royal power in France.

The judicial system.

---

[1] Gneist, *Englische Verfassungsgeschichte*, pp. 298 *et seq.*, 468 *et seq.*; and see the note at the end of this chapter.

known by the name of *cas royaux*.[1] But this process aroused serious resistance on the part of the territorial lords, and it was not until the sixteenth century that the crown judges possessed the universal authority they had obtained in England more than three hundred years earlier. So strong, in fact, did the local jealousy of the Parliament of Paris (the king's high court of justice) remain, that after the great fiefs fell into the hands of the crown, they were not placed under the jurisdiction of that tribunal, but were given independent parliaments of their own.[2] At the outbreak of the Revolution there were thirteen separate parliaments, so that every considerable province had a distinct body of magistrates.[3] Under these circumstances, the courts could not create a uniform national justice like the English common law, and although since the revolution such a uniform system has been provided by the Code, this does not strengthen the hands of the judges, but has rather the opposite tendency. In the first place, it is not their work, and hence does not redound to their glory; and secondly, by weakening the force of precedent, it diminishes the importance of judicial decisions. This review of the history of the courts of law shows

[1] Aubert, *Le Parlement de Paris de Phillippe le Bel à Charles VII.*, ch. i. sec. I. ; *Hist. du Parl. de Paris, 1250–1515*, liv. ii. ch. i.; Du Bois, *Hist. du Droit Criminel de la France*, part i. ch. i.; Esmein, *Hist. du Droit Français*, part i. tit. ii. ch. i.; *Hist. de la Proc. Crim.*, part i. tit. i. ch. i. sec. II.; ch. ii. sec. I.; Hallam, *Middle Ages*, ch. ii. part ii. 5.

[2] Du Bois, part i. ch. ii. § 2 ; Bastard d'Estang, *Les Parlements de France*, vol. i. pp. 36–38 ; Esmein, *Hist. du Droit Français*, tit. ii. ch. i. sec. I. § 2, v.

[3] For the dates of the creation of the provincial parliaments, which run from 1444 to 1775, see Bastard d'Estang, vol. i. p. 189, note, and Esmein, *ubi supra*.

clearly why they have not attained in France the same power and authority as in Anglo-Saxon countries.[1]

The French courts of law were weak because the royal authority did not come into direct contact with the people at the time when public and private law were everywhere blended, when the tone of thought was peculiarly legal, and when political power was chiefly exercised in a judicial or semi-judicial form.[2] It made itself felt at a later date, and especially as the restorer of order after the anarchy caused by the hundred years' war. Its presence brought peace and prosperity, and naturally enough the organs which it employed acquired a high degree of vigor. Now, at this period, administration, in the modern sense, was becoming important, and as the royal authority came to be exercised by commissioners or intendants who had, indeed, certain judicial powers, but whose functions were chiefly administrative,[3] the administration developed an influence and a strength which the courts have never attained. The administrative system became centralized, and grew to be the most important factor in the government.[4] All classes of the people looked to it for protection;[5] in fact, it took,

The administrative system.

---

[1] Since the Revolution, the courts have, of course, been reorganized on a centralized basis.

[2] On the relative importance attributed to law in the Middle Ages, and in later times, see Stubbs's chapters on the Characteristic Differences between Mediæval and Modern History, in his *Lectures on Med. and Mod. Hist.*

[3] Chéruel, *Dic. des Inst. de la France,* "Intendants des Provinces;" Esmein, *Hist. du Droit Français,* tit. ii. ch. v. § 2.

[4] Cf. De Tocqueville, *An. Reg. et la Rev.,* liv. ii. chs. ii. iii.

[5] De Tocqueville speaks of all classes as looking on the government as a special providence. *Id.,* ch. vi. (7th ed. pp. 100–103).

to a great extent, the place which the judiciary filled in England, and in those countries which had inherited the English principles.

This difference in the relative authority of the courts and the administration was intensified, so far as the United States and France were concerned, by the political philosophy of the last century. Montesquieu, in his "Spirit of the Laws," proclaimed the importance of separating the executive, legislative, and judicial powers, and the maxim was eagerly accepted on both sides of the Atlantic, though in very different senses.   Our ancestors, anxious to maintain the independence of the courts and the sacredness of private rights, took the principle to signify the necessity of so protecting the courts from the control or influence of the other branches of the government that they might be free to administer justice without regard to the official position of the litigants or the nature of the questions involved.   They meant to preserve the English tradition that there is only one law of the land to which every one is subject, from the humblest citizen to the highest officer.   The French, on the other hand, had acquired no great passion for law, or for the rights of the individual, and did not admit a claim on the part of any one to delay or overturn the public interests in order to get his own grievances redressed.   Moreover, they had seen the Parliament of Paris interfere with the government by refusing to register the edicts of the King; for although this tribunal had failed to acquire judicial supremacy, it had retained a good deal of political power, which it used during the years preceding the

Effect of the doctrine of the separation of powers.

Revolution to resist innovations.[1]　Such a power might not be disliked as a means of opposing an unpopular court party, but it could not be tolerated for a moment when the reins of government were seized by men who believed themselves commissioned to reform the world. The French statesmen, therefore, took Montesquieu's doctrine in the sense that the administration ought to be free to act for the public weal without let or hindrance from the courts of law. The Declaration of the Rights of Man proclaimed in 1789 that a community in which the separation of powers was not established had no constitution; and a statute of the next year, on the organization of the tribunals, gave effect to the maxim as it was understood in France by providing that the judges should not interfere in any way with the work of administrative authorities, or proceed against the officers of the government on account of their official acts.[2]　The American and French applications of the doctrine of the separation of powers are both perfectly logical, but are based on different conceptions of the nature of law.　The Anglo-Saxon draws no distinction between public and private law.　To him all legal rights and duties of every kind form part of one universal system of positive law, and so far as the functions of public officials are not regulated by that law, they are purely matters of discretion.　It follows that every legal question, whether it involves the power of a public officer or the construction of a private contract, comes

[1] Cf. Edward J. Lowell, *The Eve of the French Revolution*, p. 105.

[2] Aucoc, *Conférences*, part i. liv. i. ch. i.; Bœuf, *Résumé*, part iv. sec. II.

before the ordinary courts.[1]　In France, on the other hand, private law, or the regulation of the rights and duties of individuals among themselves, is treated as only one branch of jurisprudence; while public law, which deals with the principles of government and the relations of individuals to the state, is regarded as something of an entirely different kind.　Of course every civilized government must strive to treat all its subjects fairly, and hence, in the course of administration, questions of justice must arise; but as these do not concern the rights of a man against his neighbor, they are not classed in France with private law.　It is felt that, unlike questions of private law, they ought not to be decided solely by the application of abstract principles of justice between man and man, but must be considered from the broad standpoint of public policy. Now the domain of the ordinary French courts is private law alone, and it is quite logical to regard any attempt on their part to judge administrative acts and thus pass on questions of public policy, as an attempt to go beyond their proper sphere of action and invade the province of the executive.[2]

The principle of withdrawing questions of public law from the ordinary courts was not new.　It existed in

---

[1] This principle, like all others in Anglo-Saxon countries, is not carried out with absolute consistency.　Thus the various commissions in America on railroads, interstate commerce, etc., partake of the nature of the French administrative tribunals.

[2] The French, like the Americans, have not applied their principles quite strictly, for Criminal Law ought to be a branch of Public Law (Aucoc, Introd. § 1), but it has been put into the charge of the ordinary courts.

practice under the old régime,[1] but was extended and systematized after the Revolution. The protection of officials from suit or prosecution was formally incorporated into the Constitution of the year VIII. (1799), and remained in force until after the fall of Napoleon III., when it was repealed by a decree of the Government of the National Defense.[2] This decree was intended to remove all hindrances in the way of bringing government officials before the ordinary courts, but it had very little effect, because the Tribunal of Conflicts held that it applied only to the personal protection of officials, and did not affect the principle of the separation of powers, which, as understood in France, forbids the ordinary judges to pass upon the legality of official acts.[3] Questions of this kind, therefore, are still reserved exclusively for the administrative courts, — *The administrative courts.*

tribunals created especially for this purpose, and composed of officials in the service of the government. Criminal cases are, indeed, an exception to the rule,[4] but this is of no great practical importance, because as force is pretty sure to be on the side of the police, it is no real protection to the individual to know that he can-

[1] See Laferrière, *Traité*, liv. i. ; De Tocqueville, *An. Reg. et la Rev.*, book ii. ch. iv. ; Varagnac, " Le Conseil d'Etat," *Revue des Deux Mondes*, Aug. 15, 1892.

[2] Decree of Sept. 19, 1870.

[3] Arrêt, 30 Juillet, 1873, " Affaire Pélétier," Dalloz, *Jur. Gen.*, 1874, part iii. p. 5 ; Leferrière, *Traité*, liv. iii. ch. vii. ; Aucoc, *Conf.*, liv. v. ch. ii. ; Goodnow, *Comp. Adm. Law*, vol. ii. pp. 172–76.

[4] Laferrière, *Traité*, liv. iii. ch. vi. But even this exception is not absolute. See, also, a discussion of the subject in Dalloz, 1881, part iii. p. 17, note.

not be condemned for resistance; and on the other hand
the officials concerned run no risk of punishment for
illegal acts committed in obedience to orders, because
the government can easily manage to prevent their
being brought to trial, and can pardon them if con-
victed.   In France, therefore, there is one law for the
citizen and another for the public official, and thus
the executive is really independent of the judiciary,
for the government has always a free hand, and can
violate the law if it wants to do so without having anything to fear from the ordinary courts.   Nor is the
danger of interference on the part of the administrative
tribunals as great as it would be in the case of the
ordinary judges, because the former can be controlled
absolutely in case of necessity; and, in fact, they are
so much a part of the administration itself that they
fall into the province of the Interior and not that of
Justice.[1]   The independence of the ordinary judges is
secured by a provision which prevents their removal or
transfer to another court, without the approval of the
Court of Cassation, the final court of error.   But the

[1] It would be absurd to suppose that the government always extorts
a favorable judgment. This was clearly shown in 1895, in a once
famous case, which illustrates at the same time the degree of respect
entertained for the decisions of the administrative courts. The Minister
of the Interior and the railroads disagreed about the interpretation of a
statute relating to the state guarantee of interest on the securities of the
roads. The matter was brought before the Council of State, which
decided in favor of the railroad. Thereupon the Minister of the Interior
resigned, but the rest of the cabinet felt bound to abide by the decision.
A discussion was, however, raised in the Chamber of Deputies, which in
effect censured the ministers for submitting the matter to the Council of
State, and thereby caused the cabinet to resign.

judges of the administrative courts enjoy no such protection, and can be removed by the President at any
time.[1] The result is that, although a great mass of
administrative law has slowly grown up from the decisions of these courts,[2] and personal liberty is much
more respected than under the Empire, yet the courts
themselves cannot be considered entirely judicial bodies,
and are far from providing the rights of the citizen with
a complete guarantee, at least where political questions
are involved.[3]

[1] Aucoc, *Conf.*, vol. i. pp. 156–57; Bœuf, *Résumé*, pp. 39–40. The members of the Council of State who are qualified to sit as administrative
judges are said to be always selected from the political friends of the
government (Dupriez, *Les Ministres*, vol. ii. pp. 482–83).

[2] Unlike the civil law, the administrative law has never been codified,
and indeed it could not be without destroying the element of discretion
which is the reason for its existence. So far as it is not contained in
statutes and ordinances, it has developed, like the English Common Law,
by decision and precedent, and hence the sources for studying it are the
reported cases and the writings of jurists such as those heretofore cited.

[3] Lebon, *France as It Is*, pp. 101–2; Goodnow (*Comp. Administrative
Law*, vol. ii. pp. 220–21, 231) remarks that the administrative courts have
shown themselves more favorable to private rights than the ordinary
courts, and in some ways that is certainly true. In English-speaking
countries a public official can be prosecuted criminally or sued for damages in the ordinary courts for any acts done without legal authority,
whether his action was in the public interest or not. But he is not, as a
rule, liable for acts authorized by law although his actual motives were
bad or his discretionary powers misused. Nor is he usually liable for
negligence in the performance of his duties. The state, on the other
hand, cannot in theory be sued at all. In practice some means of maintaining claims against the state is almost always provided; but only for
breaches of contract or to recover property, not for torts committed by
officials.

In France acts of officials are classified in quite another way with very
different results. First, there are personal acts, which involve grave per-

It is evident that with two sets of courts, neither of
which is superior to the other, disputes about
jurisdiction must constantly arise. Such is in

sonal misconduct or gross negligence on the part of the official, whether
beyond or within his legal authority. For these, and these alone, he is
liable in damages in the ordinary courts. Whatever he does in good faith
for the public interest, whether within or beyond his legal authority, is an
act of administration for which a remedy, if any, can be sought only
against the state, and as a rule only in the administrative courts. Acts
of this kind fall into three classes, called, *actes de gestion, actes d'authorité*
and *actes de gouvernement*. Broadly speaking, *actes de gestion* are acts
done in the course of the business administration of the public services, and the administrative courts tend to award compensation against
the state for acts of this nature, not only when done wholly without
legal authority, but also when there has been an abuse of that authority for improper purposes, or even negligence, as, for example, where
a merchantman has been damaged by collision with a warship. (See
a discussion of this whole subject in Hauriou *La Gestion Administrative*). *Actes d'authorité* are done in the exercise of the right of the state
to issue commands to its citizens; and if such commands, orders or regulations are issued without legal authority, or involve an abuse of power,
they can be annulled by a special procedure in the Council of State, which
may incidentally award compensation. Finally *actes de gouvernement*, that
is acts done for reasons of state with a view to the public safety, whether
within the legal power of the government or not, lie beyond the jurisdiction both of the ordinary and the administrative courts; but there is a
distinct tendency to restrict this principle to an ever-narrowing field.

It is obvious that while the French system does not hold the official to
a rigid conformity with law, it often gives compensation from the public
treasury for tortious acts of officials when in England or America there
would be no redress, or only an action against an official who might be
unable to pay the damages.

It is somewhat curious in this connection to observe that French
writers often assert the inability of an ordinary court to protect the public against illegal ordinances, because it can only decide the case at bar,
whereas an administrative court has power to annul the ordinance altogether; a remark which shows an entire failure to comprehend the force
of precedent in a judicial system like that of England. (See, for example,

fact the case, and a special tribunal has been appointed
to determine these disputes, or conflicts as they are
called.[1] It is composed of the Minister of Justice, of
three members of the highest court of law, the Court of
Cassation, of three members of the highest administrative court, the Council of State (each of these sets being
selected by their own court), and of two other persons
elected by the foregoing seven. All the members are
chosen for three years, except the Minister of Justice.
This officer has the right to preside, and thus his presence gives to the administration a majority in the tribunal. A striking example of the working of the system was presented in 1880, when the government issued
decrees for the suppression of all monastic orders not
authorized by law. There seems to have been grave
doubt about the legality of the decrees, and the victims
brought suits in the ordinary courts in several parts of
France. Most of these courts held that they were
authorized to entertain the suits, and in some cases they
went so far as to order the persons who had been expelled from their establishments to be restored to possession pending the trial ;[2] but the government raised
the question of jurisdiction, and the Tribunal of Con-

Varagnac, "Le Conseil d'Etat," *Revue des Deux Mondes*, Sept. 15, 1892,
pp. 290–91.)

An admirable comparison of the English and French systems may be
found in Professor Dicey's *Law of the Constitution*, and especially in
chapter xii.

[1] Aucoc, *Conf.*, vol. i. § 406; Bœuf, *Résumé*, 15th ed. pp. 542–43.

[2] Some of the decisions to this effect may be found in Dalloz, *Jurisprudence Générale*, 1880, part iii. pp. 57–62, and 80. In the note to page 57
there is a list of some of the other similar decisions and a discussion of
the law.

flicts decided that the ordinary courts were not compe-
tent to deal with the matter.[1] It is a significant fact,
which seems to show a lack of confidence in the impar-
tiality of the administrative courts, that the persons
injured did not bring the question of the legality of
the decrees before the Council of State.[2]

When an ordinary court has assumed jurisdiction of
a case, the question of competence can be raised only
by the prefect, and not by a party, for the principle
that the ordinary courts cannot determine the legality
of official acts is intended solely as a protection to the
administration.[3]

It is not quite accurate to say that the ordinary
Jurisdiction courts can consider the validity of no official
of the ad- act, and, indeed, the line between the juris-
ministrative
courts. diction of the ordinary and the administrative
courts does not follow any strictly logical principle.[4]
Questions of indirect taxes, for example, and those
relating to the lesser highways (*petite voirie*), come
before the ordinary courts, while those arising under
the direct taxes, or relating to the greater highways
(*grande voirie*), come before the administrative tribunals. The competence of the various administrative

[1] Arrêts de Nov. 4, 5, 13, 17, and 20 ; Dalloz, 1880, part iii. pp. 121–
32. These cases are reported with unusual fullness.

[2] At least I can find no decision on the subject by the Council of State
reported in Dalloz. For criticisms on the conduct of the government,
see Jules Simon, *Dieu, Patrie, Liberté*, ch. vi. ; and Channes, *Nos Fautes*,
letters of July 12 and Oct. 27, 1880.

[3] Aucoc, *Conf.*, vol. i. § 404; Bœuf, *Résumé*, 15th ed. p. 547.

[4] On this subject, see Laferrière's great work, *Traité de la Jurisdiction
Administrative*.

courts is no less complicated. The prefect and the mayor have each a very limited jurisdiction. That of the prefectorial councils, on the other hand, is very considerable, although as a matter of fact these councils are occupied almost altogether with questions of taxes, and in these, as a rule, they follow the advice of the assessors.[1] But by far the most important administrative court is the Council of State, which has a special section or committee to attend to the *contentieux*, as this class of litigation is called. The Council not only hears appeals from the lower administrative tribunals, but has also original jurisdiction in many important cases, and in fact recent practice is tending to establish the principle that the Council of State is the judge of all administrative matters in the absence of special provisions of law. The number of cases brought before it is very large, and has increased so rapidly that the section for the *contentieux* is badly in arrears, and it has been proposed to create a second section to relieve the pressure.[2]

Such is the legal position of the administration in ordinary times, but in case of war or insurrection it can be given far greater powers, by a proclamation of the state of siege. This can be made by statute, or if Parliament is not in session, it can be made by the President; but in that case, in order to meet the danger of a *coup d'état*, which is ever present

The state of siege.

---

[1] Vicomte d'Avenel, "La Réforme Administrative — La Justice," *Revue des Deux Mondes*, June 1, 1889, p. 596.

[2] For the number of cases decided by the administrative courts, see the tables (through 1886) in Laferrière, liv. i. ch. v.

to the eyes of Frenchmen, it is provided that the Chambers shall meet as of right in two days.[1] Within the
district covered by the state of siege, the military courts
can be given criminal jurisdiction, and can punish any
offenses against the safety of the Republic or the general
peace. They can search houses by day or night, expel
from the district any non-residents, seize all arms, and
forbid any publications or meetings which are liable to
disturb the public order.[2]

Effect of the French system on the position of the executive.
  I have dwelt at some length on what, from an
Anglo-Saxon point of view, may well be called
the legislative and judicial powers of the
executive in France, because these things are
entirely foreign to our own political ideas and
experience, and because they exist in some form in
almost every country on the continent of Europe.

When we consider the paternal character of the
government, the centralization of the state, and the
large share of authority vested in the executive department, we cannot fail to see that the ministers in whose
hands this vast power is lodged must be either very
strong or very weak. If they are able to wield it as
they please, and are really free to carry out their own
policy, they must be far stronger than any officer or
body in Great Britain, and immeasurably stronger than
any in our federal republic. But, on the other hand,
the very immensity and pervasiveness of their power,
the fact that it touches closely every interest in the
country, renders them liable to pressure from all sides.

[1] Law of April 3, 1878, Poudra et Pierre, § 79.
[2] Poudra et Pierre, § 76, gives the text of the law.

It becomes important for every one to influence their action, provided he can get a standpoint from which to bring a pressure to bear. This standpoint is furnished by the Chamber of Deputies, for the existence of the ministry depends on the votes of that body. The greater, therefore, the power of the minister, and the more numerous the favors he is able to bestow, the fiercer will be the struggle for them, and the less will he be free to pursue his own policy, untrammeled by deputies, whose votes he must win if he would remain in office. A Frenchman, who is eminent as a student of political philosophy, and has at the same time great practical experience in politics, once remarked to the author, " We have the organization of an empire with the forms of a republic." [1] The French administrative system is, indeed, designed for an empire, and would work admirably in the hands of a wise and benevolent autocrat who had no motive but the common weal; but when arbitrary power falls under the control of popular leaders, it can hardly fail to be used for personal and party ends; for, as a keen observer has truly said, the defect of democracy lies in the fact that it is nobody's business to look after the interests of the public.[2]

[1] Gneist expresses the same idea : " *Es entsteht der unvermittelte Gegensatz einer republikanisch gedachten Verfassung mit einer absolutistisch organisirten Verwaltung.*" (*Die Preussische Kreisordnung*, p. 7.)

[2] The late Professor Gneist, perhaps the most profound student of the comparative history of England and the continent, from the point of view of the working of parliamentary government, demonstrated that the success of the system in England has been due to certain underlying institutions which have made that country a commonwealth based upon law (*Rechtsstaat*). His chief works on the subject are his *Englische Verwaltungsrecht ; Self-government, etc., in England; Der Rechtsstaat,* and

Verwaltung, Justiz, Rechtsweg. In the opening words of the preface to
the last of these, the keynote of the whole theory is struck when he says,
" *Die parlamentarische Regierung Englands ist eine Regierung nach Gesetzen
und durch Gesetze.*"

His views may be briefly summarized as follows : In England alone,
among the countries of Europe, the royal power became consolidated
early, for the Norman kings broke down the resistance of the great
vassals and made their authority effective over the whole realm, drawing
military, judicial, and police matters into their own hands. By this
process, the antagonism and jealousy of the different classes was crushed ;
while the land-owning nobility found their only chance of political activity
in exerting a restraint upon the crown by means of judicial action and
statutes. Their first great achievement was Magna Charta, with which the
parliamentary era begins. The struggle was continued in the Barons'
war, and resulted in the evolution of the House of Commons.

From time to time Parliament enacted statutes which supplemented
the customary law, and furnished a solid basis for the decisions of the
courts. The existence of permanent statutes, as distinguished from royal
edicts in their nature changeable, is one of the chief foundations of the
reign of law in England, for the statutes in ever increasing quantity regulated the administration rigorously and uniformly throughout the land.

Another factor that contributed to the same result was the method in
which the statutes were executed, and this in turn may be traced to the
early extension of the royal power. The administrative laws were
carried out by means of a large number of officers, of whom the most
important were the justices of the peace. These were appointed by the
king, and hence acted in behalf of the state instead of local or class
interests ; but, on the other hand, they were in fact the greater landowners of the county, not professional officials bound to do the bidding of
the court. They conducted the local administration according to judicial
forms, subject on purely legal questions to the control of the King's
Bench by means of writs of *Certiorari, Mandamus,* etc., the effect being to
prevent arbitrary abuse of power, and to insure legality in the execution
of the law. In short, as Gneist expresses it, the English developed an
elaborate and effective system of administrative justice.

The method of administration also produced self-government, by which
Gneist means not the control of local matters by bodies elected to represent local interests, but an organization of the whole community for the
service of the state, so arranged that the classes most capable by their
wealth and position for government bore the burdens and administered
the affairs of their neighborhood. The result was brought about in

England chiefly by means of the office of justice of the peace, which gradually became both an honor and a duty attached to the ownership of land. Thus the gentry carried on the local government ; but this was no mere privilege which they enjoyed for their own benefit, because they also paid the taxes and ruled, not for the profit of their own class, but as officers of the state for the common good and in strict accordance with fixed laws. Hence, instead of the hostility of classes that existed all over the continent, there developed harmonious local communities with true public opinions on political questions. Moreover, the habit of sitting as justices gave to the gentry a sense of public duty and a love for law. Now the House of Commons was virtually composed of the representatives of the gentry, who carried into it their sentiments. The members of Parliament, therefore, understood law, and had a deep sense of its importance, while their training caused them to act for the good of the whole state rather than the benefit of their own class. This rendered possible the formation of real national parties, based on differences of opinion, not on class interests ; parties whose action in Parliament was restricted by a respect for law.

Gneist points out how different has been the history of France. Feudalism there was at first too strong for the royal power to overcome, and hence the community, instead of being consolidated, split into hostile classes. The king found himself at the head of a state whose organization was so loose and inefficient as to be incapable of natural development. As soon as he was able, he began to create in the royal domains better military, financial, police, and judicial systems. The old institutions having gained no strength in the mean while were unable to stand against the new and more effective ones, which gradually spread over the whole of France. The new ones, however, were not combined with the old, but substituted for them ; and thus the power both of the vassals and of the estates was crushed by the royal supremacy. In fact, the political and social organization of the country became entirely unlike. Socially, the nation was still divided into the classes whose selfish antagonism had made possible the triumph of the crown. Politically, absolute power had become vested in the king, who ruled by means of a paid corps of officials without ties with the local communities, unrestrained by permanent statutes, and dependent solely on his pleasure. The French Revolution did not essentially change this state of things. It did not create a new organic political structure of the community, but merely transferred the royal power to the people, or rather to those particular interests among the people that were able to acquire ascendency for the moment, and these were no more inclined to place restraints on their own omnipotence than the king had been before. While, therefore, private law was just and strong, public law was weak and unstable ; and as public law is the foundation of political society, Gneist regards France as the very negation of a commonwealth based upon law.

German history followed very much the same course during the Middle Ages, but at their close the central power was not strong enough to enforce obedience and consolidate the empire. Hence the supremacy of the crown developed at a still later time, after the centrifugal forces had grown so powerful that the principalities had become well-nigh independent. Then the princes overcame within their territories the resistance of the estates as the king had done in France. In Germany, however, and especially in Prussia, the bureaucracy was so ordered as to furnish a better protection to individual rights and a firmer maintenance of law. But this broke down with the spread of French ideas after 1848, when the antagonistic interests in the state, taking advantage of the parliamentary system, abused the administrative power and introduced a veritable party tyranny.

Gneist considered the subsidiary framework of the English institutions, and especially the justices of the peace, as the foundation of the legal character of the government, and hence of the success of the parliamentary system. But he did not realize that the keystone of the whole structure is the ultimate decision by the courts at Westminster of all questions of law that arise in the course of the administration. He did not see that the legal spirit pervading the system is the result of giving to public law the sacredness and inflexibility that pertains to private law, and that this end is reached by fusing the two together, and confiding them both in the last resort to the same courts. On the contrary, he believed that public and private law ought to be kept distinct, and he approved of the practice of placing the former in the hands of special administrative tribunals. The germs of such a system appeared for a moment in England when the Star Chamber began to act as a supreme administrative court ; but one cannot help feeling that if this procedure had become permanent, public law would have been much less rigidly interpreted than it was by the King's Bench, that the administration would have become more discretionary, and that the strict, rigorous, legal spirit of the system would have been lost.

It may be added that Gneist considered the English government at its highest perfection under George III. In his opinion, the reform bill of 1832, the extension of the franchise in 1867, and still more the recent changes in local government, have been a departure from historic principles, and have tended by disorganizing the state to bring about a strife of parties and reduce England to the condition of other nations.

CHAPTER II.

FRANCE: PARTIES.

For more than a hundred years it has been the habit to talk of government by the people, and the expression is, perhaps, more freely used to-day than ever before, yet a superficial glance at the history of democracy ought to be enough to convince us that in a great nation the people as a whole do not and cannot really govern. The fact is that we are ruled by parties, whose action is more or less modified, but never completely directed, by public opinion. Rousseau, indeed, shadowed forth a great truth, when he declared that no community could be capable of a general will — or as we should express it, of a true public opinion — where parties or sects prevailed;[1] and our own experience of popular government will quite justify us in saying that public opinion is always more or less warped by the existence of party ties. A study of the nature and development of parties is, therefore, the most important one that can occupy the student of political philosophy to-day. Among Anglo-Saxon peoples, who have had a far longer experience in self-government than most other races, there are usually two great parties which dispute for mastery in the

The influence of parties in popular government.

As a rule there are only two parties in Anglo-Saxon countries, but several elsewhere.

[1] *Contrat Social,* liv. ii. ch. iii.

state. But in the countries on the continent of Europe this is not usually true. We there find a number of parties or groups which are independent of each other to a greater or less extent, and form coalitions, sometimes of a most unnatural kind, to support or oppose the government of the hour. Now the existence of several distinct political groups has a decisive influence on the working of the parliamentary system. Let us consider this question a moment.

When a country with a parliamentary form of government is divided into two hostile parties, the ministers who lead the majority of the popular chamber must of course belong all to one of those parties, or all to the other, and they are forced by circumstances to work in harmony.

Under the parliamentary system there are normally only two parties.

But even when party strife is less bitter, and parties have begun to break up, experience has proved that the best policy for the ministers is to support each other and stand or fall together. Lord Melbourne is reported to have exclaimed at a cabinet meeting, after a discussion on the question of changing the duty on corn, " Now is it to lower the price of corn, or is n't it? It is not much matter which we say, but mind, we must all say the same." [1] The statesmanship implied by this remark may not have been of the highest kind, but the politics were sound, and showed a knowledge of the great secret of success. It is, indeed, an axiom in politics that, except under very peculiar circumstances, coalition ministries are short-lived compared with homogeneous ones, whose members are in

[1] Bagehot, *English Constitution*, p. 16, note.

cordial sympathy with each other. Now so long as the
ministers cling together, every member of the House
must consider the cabinet and its policy as a whole, and
make up his mind whether he will support it, or help
to turn it out and put in an entirely different set of
ministers with another policy. He cannot support the
cabinet on certain questions and oppose it on others.
He must sacrifice details to the general question. The
result is that the members either group themselves
about the ministers, and vote with them through thick
and thin, or else they attach themselves to an opposition party, whose object is to turn out the cabinet, and
then take office itself and carry on a different policy.
The normal condition of the parliamentary system,
therefore, among a people sufficiently free from prejudices to group themselves naturally, and possessing
enough experience to know that the practical and
attainable, and not the ideal, is the true aim in politics,
is a division into two parties, each of which is ready to
take office whenever the other loses its majority. This
has been true in England in ordinary times, and
although of late years it has been frequently asserted
that the two great parties in the House of Commons
are destined to come to an end, and be replaced by a
number of independent groups, the prophecy does not
accord with experience. It is based on the state of the
Parliament of 1892, and seems to arise from mistaking
a temporary political condition for a permanent one. The
sudden interjection of the question of Home Rule into
English politics caused a new party division on fresh
lines, which necessarily broke up the traditional associ-

ations of public life, and threw both parties into a state
of confusion that has not yet disappeared. On one
side, the opponents of the measure were composed of
men whose habits of thought had been most diverse ;
while the followers of Mr. Gladstone, on the other side,
included many Liberals who were forced, against their
will, to subordinate to Home Rule other matters which
they deemed more important. In short, the introduction of a new issue shattered the old basis of cleavage,
and it is not surprising that new, solidified parties were
not formed in an instant. Moreover it may be noticed
that although the Liberal groups in the late House of
Commons talked freely of their dissensions, they acted
as a single party, and supported the cabinet by their
votes with astonishing fidelity.

A division into two parties is not only the normal
result of the parliamentary system, but also
an essential condition of its success. Suppose, for example, that a third party, like that

It cannot
work well
otherwise.

of the Irish Home Rulers under Parnell, is formed, and
places some one specific issue above all others, with the
determination of voting against any cabinet that does
not yield to its demands on that point ; and suppose
this body becomes large enough to hold the balance
of power. If, in such a case, the two old parties do
not make a coalition, or one of them does not absorb
the new group by making concessions, no ministry will
be able to secure a majority. Every cabinet will be
overthrown as soon as it is formed, and parliamentary
government will be an impossibility. Now suppose that
the third party, instead of being implacably hostile to

both the others, is willing for a time to tolerate a cabinet from one of them, — is willing, in short, to allow the ministers to retain office provided they give no offense. Under these circumstances parliamentary government is not impossible, but it is extremely difficult. The ministers are compelled to ride two horses at once. They must try to conciliate two inharmonious bodies of men, on pain of defeat if either of them becomes hostile; and hence their tenure is unstable and their course necessarily timid. Now the larger the number of discordant groups that form the majority, the harder the task of pleasing them all, and the more feeble and unstable the position of the cabinet. Nor is the difficulty removed by giving portfolios to the members of the several groups; for even if this reduces the labor of satisfying the parties, it adds that of maintaining an accord among the ministers themselves, and entails the proverbial weakness of coalition governments. A cabinet which depends for its existence on the votes of the Chamber can pursue a consistent policy with firmness and effect only when it can rely for support on a compact and faithful majority; and therefore the parliamentary system will give the country a strong and efficient government only in case the majority consists of a single party. But this is not all. The opposition must also be united. So long as the ministry stands, the composition of the minority is, indeed, of little consequence; but when that minority becomes a majority, it must in turn be a single party, or the weakness of a coalition ministry cannot be avoided. It follows that a division of the Chamber into two parties, and two par-

ties only, is necessary in order that the parliamentary
form of government should permanently produce good
results.

In France the parliamentary system has not worked
well, because this condition has not been fulfilled.[1] The various groups of Monarchists
and Bonapartists have together formed in the
Chambers the party of the Reactionaries, or
as it is more commonly called, the Right.[2]   The rest of

This condi-
tion has not
been ful-
filled in
France.

---

[1] This is recognized by many French writers, e. g., Lamy, *La République en 1883;* Paul Laffitte, *Le Suffrage Universel et la Régime Parlementaire,*
pt. i. ch. iii. ; Saleilles, in the *Annals of the American Academy of Political
Science,* July, 1895, pp. 57, 64, 65. But the reason for the existence of a
number of groups in France seems to be only partially understood. The
most clear-sighted writer on this subject is Dupriez. (See *Les Ministres,*
vol. ii. pp. 363–65, 370–71, and 386–95.)

[2] For readers unfamiliar with European politics it may perhaps be
necessary to explain the meaning of the terms Right and Left, as they
are used all over the Continent. In England a broad aisle runs from the
Speaker's desk through the middle of the House of Commons to the main
entrance opposite, and the benches of the members are arranged parallel
to this aisle and facing it. The Ministry sit on the front bench at the
right of the Speaker (the so-called Treasury Bench), their supporters
taking seats behind and alongside of them, while the opposition sit on the
left side of the House. The Liberals and Conservatives, therefore, are
each to be found sometimes on one side of the House and sometimes on
the other, according as their party is in power or not. But on the Continent the seats are arranged, as a rule, like those of a theatre, as in our
legislative bodies, the ministers usually sitting immediately in front of
the Speaker or President, on a bench which sometimes faces him and
sometimes looks the other way, while the conservative members sit on
the President's right, the more liberal next to these, and the radical on
his left. As this arrangement is permanent, the words Right and Left
have come to be generally used for Conservative and Liberal ; and the
different groups are often designated by their position in the Chamber,
as the Right, the Centre, and the Left Centre, the Left, or the Extreme
Left.

the members have been supporters of the Republic, and have formed nominally a single party, but they have really been held together only by a desire to maintain the existing form of government, and have seldom acted in concert except when they thought that threatened. They have always comprised men of every shade of opinion, from conservatives to radicals and even socialists, and would speedily have broken up into completely hostile parties, if it had not been for the fear of the Reactionaries. Even under the pressure of this fear their cohesion has been very slight, for they have been divided into a number of groups with organizations which, though never either complete or durable, have been quite separate; and again, these groups have often been subdivided into still smaller groups, whose members were loosely held together by similarity of opinions or desire for advancement, usually under the standard of some chief, who held, or hoped to win, a place in the cabinet. In fact, the parties in the Chamber of Deputies have presented such a series of dissolving views that it is very difficult to draw an intelligible picture of them.[1]

[1] The line of cleavage between the monarchists and republicans has now ceased to be of much importance. All the larger factions now profess to be republican. These factions are constantly gaining or losing members so that it is almost impossible to state their exact numerical strength at any one time. Sometimes it happens, indeed, that a member of the Chamber may profess to belong to two political groups at the same time. No single faction ever forms a majority of the Chamber so that a coalition or *bloc* is necessary. The following groups at present make up the Chamber of Deputies but their names afford, for the most part, no indication of the principles to which they give allegiance : Conservatives (or members of the extreme Right) ; Nationalists (members of the Action Libérale

During the struggle with MacMahon, the Republicans had been solidly united, but the danger had not passed very long before the Radicals began to show themselves independent. They soon became quite ready to upset any ministry that offended them, and in fact cabinet after cabinet was overthrown by the votes of the Right and the Extreme Left. Even Gambetta, who had striven to keep the Republicans together, did not escape this fate, in spite of his immense popularity both in the country and in the Parliament. He did not consent to form a ministry until November, 1881; and after holding office only two months and a half, he was forced to resign by the refusal of the Chamber to introduce the *scrutin de liste* for the election of deputies. He lived only till the end of the year, and his death deprived France of her only great popular leader. After his fall, politics followed the old course, and there passed across the stage a series of short-lived ministries.

During the last few years there has indeed been a nearer approach to a division of the deputies into two great parties — one Conservative and the other Radical — than at any other time since the birth of the Republic; and yet the history of the successive ministries during the life of the later Chambers makes it clear with how little sharpness the lines are drawn, and how little the members of the various groups

populaire); Progressives; Republicans (or Moderates); Radicals; Radical-Socialists; Independent Socialists; and Independents. The first three groups make up the *Right;* the last five usually make up the *Left;* but some of the smaller groups keep shifting from side to side.

that compose the majority can be relied upon to be faithful to the cabinet. In short, there has been an approach to the system of two parties, but as yet not a very near approach, and the numerous detached groups still remain the basis of parliamentary life.

Let us now consider the reasons for the subdivisions of the Chamber into a number of groups. And first we must look at a source of political dissensions with which we are not familiar at home, but which is to be found in almost every nation in Europe.

Causes of the existence of many parties in France.

Few persons ever ask themselves why the bodies of men who assemble every year at the State House or the Capitol have power to make laws. It is not because they have more personal force or wisdom or virtue than any one else. A congress of scientific men may contain all these qualities in greater abundance, but it cannot change a single line in the statute-book. Is it because they represent the people? But we all know that they occasionally pass laws which the people do not want, and yet we obey those laws without hesitation. Moreover, this answer only pushes the question one step further back, for why should we obey the people? A few centuries ago nobody recognized any right on the part of the people to govern or misgovern themselves as they chose, or rather on the part of the majority to impose their will on the minority; and in many countries of the world no such right is recognized to-day. How does it happen that there is not a class of men among us who

The lack of a political consensus.

think that the legislature does not fairly represent the people, or who think that the right to vote ought to be limited by a certain educational or property qualification, or by the profession of a certain creed; and why does not some such class of men get up a rival legislature? The fact is that, while we may differ in regard to the ideal form of government, we are all of one mind on the question of what government is entitled to our actual allegiance, and we are all determined to yield to that government our obedience and support. In short, a common understanding or consensus in regard to the basis and form of the government is so universal here that we feel as if it were natural and inevitable; but in all countries this is not so. Such a consensus is the foundation of all political authority, of all law and order; and it is easy to see that if it were seriously questioned, the position of the government would be shaken, that if it were destroyed, the country would be plunged into a state of anarchy. Now persons who do not accept the consensus on which the political authority of the day is based are termed in France Irreconcilables. Men of this sort do not admit the rightfulness of the existing government, and although they may submit to it for the moment, their object is to effect a revolution by peaceful if not by violent means. Hence their position is essentially different from that of all other parties, for these aim only at directing the policy of the government within constitutional limits, and can be intrusted with power without danger to the fundamental institutions of the nation, while the Irreconcilables, on the contrary, would use their power to upset those institutions, and therefore cannot be suffered to get control of the state. They form an opposition that is incapable of taking office, and so present a disturbing element, which in a parliamentary form of government throws the whole system out of gear.[1]

Another thing to be noticed about a consensus is that it cannot be created artificially, but must be the result of a slow growth and long traditions. Its essence lies in the fact that it is unconscious. The people of the United States, for example, could not, by agreement, give to a dictator the power the Czar wields in Russia, for except in the presence of imminent danger he would have no authority unless the people believed in his inherent right to rule, and the people cannot make themselves believe in any such right simply by agreeing to do so. The foundation of government is faith, not reason, and the faith of a people is not vital unless they have been born with it.[2] Now,

A consensus cannot be created rapidly.

The French Revolution destroyed every political consensus.

---

[1] It is impossible to draw a sharp line between what is revolutionary and what is not; or to define exactly an Irreconcilable. The matter depends in fact upon the opinion of the community. Thus, before 1886, Home Rule might fairly be said to have been revolutionary, and the Irish Home Rulers to have been Irreconcilables; but after Mr. Gladstone made Home Rule a practical question in English politics, it would have been absurd to call Parnell's followers Irreconcilables.

[2] Curiously enough an exception to this principle, and almost a solitary one, is to be found in the history of the United States. The generation that framed the Constitution looked upon that document as very imperfect, but they clung to it tenaciously as the only defense against national dismemberment, and in order to make it popular, they praised it beyond their own belief in its merits. This effort to force themselves to admire the Constitution was marvelously successful, and resulted, in the

in France, the Revolution of 1789 destroyed all faith in the political institutions of the past, and was unable to substitute anything else. It did, indeed, give birth to a code of law, and to an administrative system, both of which have taken a strong hold on the nation, and have survived every change in the government. These are the permanent elements in France, and the only ones that have acquired the blind force of tradition. They supply a machinery that is unshaken by political upheavals, and it is this that has made it possible for the country to pass through so many revolutions without falling into a state of anarchy.[1] But in regard to institutions of a purely political character, the nation has not been so fortunate, for the governments that followed the Revolution were not sufficiently durable to lay even a foundation for a general consensus, and the lack of continuity has so thoroughly prevented the steady growth of opinion that the people have not succeeded in acquiring a political creed. The result is that every form of government that has existed in France has its partisans, who are irreconcilable under every other; while the great mass of the middle classes and the peasants have no strong political convictions, and are ready to support any government that maintains order. Thus the two Empires bequeathed to the Republic the group of Bonapartists, while the Monarchists are a legacy from the old régime and the reign of Louis Philippe. At pres-

The effect of this on parties.

next generation, in a worship of the Constitution, of which its framers never dreamed.

[1] Cf. Laffitte, pp. 208, 209.

ent it seems altogether probable that, if no great European crisis occurs, the Right will end by accepting the Republic, and if so the irreconcilable elements will disappear or become insignificant, and one of the chief obstacles to the formation of two great parties, one Conservative and the other Radical, will be removed.

But this is only one of several obstacles, and the others are so great that it will probably be a long time before the system of groups breaks down in France, or is replaced by that of two political parties.

Other causes of the sub-division of parties.

In the first place, the Frenchman is theoretical rather than practical in politics. He is inclined to pursue an ideal, striving to realize his conception of a perfect form of society, and is reluctant to give up any part of it for the sake of attaining so much as lies within his reach. Such a tendency naturally gives rise to a number of groups, each with a separate ideal, and each unwilling to make the sacrifice that is necessary for a fusion into a great party. In short, the intensity of political sentiment prevents the development of real political issues. To the Frenchman, public questions have an absolute rather than a relative or practical bearing, and therefore he cares more for principles and opinions than for facts. This tendency is shown in the programmes of the candidates, which are apt to be philosophic documents instead of statements of concrete policy, and, although published at great length, often give a comparatively small idea of the position of the author on

Theoretical character of French political opinions.

the immediate questions of the day.[1] It is shown also in the newspapers, and the use that is made of them. An Anglo-Saxon reads the newspapers chiefly for information about current events, and as all the papers contain very much the same news, he habitually reads only one. But the French papers contain far less news, and as the Frenchman reads them largely for the sake of the editorials, he commonly reads several in order to compare the opinions they express.

It is partly on account of this mental attitude, and partly owing to the absence of the habit of self-government, and the lack of sympathy between different parts of the country, that the French do not organize readily in politics. This is the more curious because in military matters they organize more easily than any other people in the world; and it is no doubt the military instinct, as well as the want of confidence in their own power of political organization, that disposes them to seek a leader and follow him blindly after he has won their confi-

The French do not organize readily in politics.

---

[1] Lebon, *France as It Is*, p. 85.

Abstracts of all the electoral programmes issued by the successful candidates for the Chamber of Deputies at the elections of 1889 and 1893, together with the results of the ballots, have been published by Duguet, under the title *Les Députés et les Cahiers Electoraux*. These volumes are very instructive; and a perusal of them shows that the programmes of the Radicals are much longer and less vague than the others, but often demand measures which lie out of the domain of practical politics, such as revision of the Constitution, abolition of the Senate, abolition of state aid to the churches, confiscation of all ecclesiastical property, elective judiciary, etc. The programmes give a very good idea of the candidate's general turn of mind; and those of the Radicals may be said to contain their conception of the ideal state of politics or of society. The Radicals are, indeed, the only group among

dence.[1] The inability to organize readily in politics
has this striking result, that vehement as some of the
groups are, and passionate as is their attachment to
their creeds, they make little effort to realize their aims,
by associating together their supporters in all parts of
the country for concerted action. In fact, there may
be said to be no national party organizations in France.[2]
The various groups into which the deputies are divided
have, as a rule, no existence whatever outside of Parliament, the candidates for seats merely calling themselves in general terms, Moderates, Radicals, Socialists,
or simply Republicans without further qualification, and
attaching themselves to a particular group after the
Chamber has met. Moreover, the programmes, which
are drawn up by each candidate for himself, are only
individual confessions of faith, and are all different, so
that there is no policy which any party as a whole is
pledged to support. Before the opening of the cam
paign, indeed, party gatherings or banquets take place,
and speeches are made, but until recent elections, no
common platform of principles has been issued except
by the Socialists.[3] It is after the campaign has begun,
however, that the absence of party organization is most
clearly seen. Then the struggle is conducted in each

the Republicans that can be said to have anything like a positive programme, and this is the source both of their strength and their weakness.

[1] Cf. Channes, Letter of Aug. 22, 1885.

[2] Cf. Lebon, *France as It Is*, p. 75 ; Theodore Stanton in the *North
American Rev.*, vol. 155, p. 471. This contrasts strangely with the United
States, where the machinery of a party has sometimes shown more
vitality than its principles.

[3] Daniel, *L'Année Politique*, 1893, pp. 254–80.

electoral district with very little regard to the rest of the country, and in fact each district appears like a separate nation engaged in a distinct contest of its own.[1] Political effort becomes localized, and except for the candidates themselves, who confine their labors to their constituencies, scarcely a man of prominence opens his mouth.

One might suppose that, under a parliamentary form of government, party organization would hardly be required, and that, as in England, the need of political cohesion would be to a great extent supplied by a strong ministry that really led Parliament and the nation.

Effect of the French political mechanism in splitting up the parties.

But here we meet with some of the other causes that tend to produce a multiplicity of groups, — causes that spring from certain of the minor French institutions which were referred to in the beginning of the first chapter as inconsistent with the parliamentary system. Three of these are especially important, — the method of electing deputies, the system of committees in the Chambers, and the practice of interpellations.

In France the *scrutin de liste,* or the election of all the deputies from a department on one ticket, and the *scrutin d'arrondissement,* or the use of single electoral districts, have prevailed alternately, the latter being in force at the present day.[2]

The method of electing deputies.

But under both systems an absolute majority of all the votes cast is required for election. If there are more than two candidates in the field, and no one of them

---

[1] Comte de Chaudordy, *La France en 1889,* p. 89.
[2] See, however, note on p. 17, *ante.*

gets such a majority, a second vote, called the *ballotage*, is taken two weeks later, and at this a plurality is enough to elect.[1]   Now it is clear that such a procedure encourages each political group to nominate a separate candidate for the first ballot.   Suppose, for example, that there are Reactionary and Moderate Republican candidates in the field, and that the Radicals prefer the Republican to the Reactionary, still they have nothing to lose by running a candidate of their own on the first ballot, for if the Reactionary can poll more votes than both his rivals combined, he will be elected in any event; if he cannot, he will not be elected whether the Radicals put up a candidate of their own or not.   In this last case, the first ballot will have counted for nothing, and the Radicals will be able to vote for the Moderate Republican at the *ballotage*, and elect him then.   They are likely, indeed, to gain a positive advantage by nominating a separate candidate, for if they succeed in polling a large vote on the first ballot, they are in an excellent position to wring concessions from the Moderates as a price of their support.

[1] Law of June 16, 1885, Art. 5.   (This article was not repealed by the Law of Feb. 13, 1889.)   By the same article a quarter as many votes as there are voters registered is required for election on the first ballot.

According to strict parliamentary usage, the term *ballotage* is applied only to cases where, at the final trial, the voting is confined by law to the two names highest on the poll at the preceding ballot, but the word is popularly used for any final ballot where a plurality is decisive.

For the choice of a senator by the electoral college of a department, the votes of a quarter of the college, and a majority of all the votes actually cast, are required on the first two ballots, while on the third a plurality is enough.   Law of August 2, 1875, Art. 15.   The election of delegates to the college by the municipal councils is conducted in the same manner.   Law of Dec. 9, 1884, Art. 8.

Cumbrous as it is, this system of voting dates back to the election of the States General in 1789, and, with a couple of short breaks, has been maintained in France ever since.[1] The idea that a representative ought to be the choice of a majority of the people seems, indeed, to be natural in democracies, for we find it put in practice elsewhere. Thus, in the United States, a majority vote was formerly very commonly required for election, but it is instructive to notice that it was found to hinder the smooth working of two political parties, and has been generally though not quite universally abandoned.[2] The fact that election by majority did not give rise to a multiplicity of parties in America shows that by itself it does not produce that result, where the other influences favor the development of two parties; but it is nevertheless clear that where a number of groups exist, it tends to foster them, and prevent their fusing into larger bodies.[3] The French system has been praised on the ground that it saves the people from the yoke of huge party machines, and

[1] Poudra et Pierre, liv. ii. ch. vii.

[2] Stimson, Am. Statute Law, § 232. In Massachusetts, election by plurality was introduced in 1855. Const. of Mass., Amendments, Art. xiv. For the previous law, see Const. pt. ii. ch. i. sec. ii. Art. iv.; ch. ii. sec. i. Art. iii.; sec. ii, Art. i.; Rev. Stats. ch. iv. sec. xiii.

[3] At the elections of 1885, which were held under the system of *scrutin de liste*, there were two Republican lists of candidates in almost all the departments. G. Channes, Letter of Oct. 30, 1885. At the elections of 1889 and 1893, held under the *scrutin d'arrondissement*, there were two Republican candidates in a large proportion of the districts, the total number of candidates for a single seat running as high as ten. Duguet, *Les Députés et les Cahiers Electoraux en 1889; Id.*, 1893. And see *Tableau des Elections à la Chambre des Députés, dressé aux Archives de la Chambre.*

enables them to select their candidates more freely.[1] This is true, and it is a great advantage. But the converse is also true; the system tends to prevent the formation of great consolidated parties, and that is the evil from which parliamentary government suffers in France to-day.[2]

The system of committees in the Chambers is a still more important matter. Each of the French chambers is divided into sections called *Bureaux*, of which there are nine in the Senate and eleven in the Chamber of Deputies.[3] The Bureaux are of equal size, and every member of the Chamber belongs to one and only one of them, the division being made afresh every month by lot. This is a very old institution in France, a relic of a time before parliamentary government had been thought of; for not only do we find it in the Assembly of Notables and the States General that met on the eve of the Revolution,[4] but it

The system of committees in the Chambers.

[1] Alfred Naquet, "The French Electoral System," in the *North Am. Rev.*, vol. 155, pp. 467–68.

[2] It is not a little curious that just at this time, when the English system of two parties is thought by many people to be in danger of breaking up, a motion should be made in the House of Commons to introduce election by majority vote and second ballot. Such a motion was made by Mr. Dalziel on April 5, 1895.

[3] For the constitution of the Bureaux and the election of the committees, see Poudra et Pierre, liv. v. chs. ii. and iii.; Reginald Dickinson, *Summary of the Constitution and Procedure of Foreign Parliaments*, 2d ed. pp. 363–66.

These Bureaux must not be confounded with the Bureau of the Chamber, which consists of the President, the Vice-Presidents, and the Secretaries. The habit in France of using the same word with different meanings is liable to be the source of no little confusion to the students of her institutions.

[4] Poudra et Pierre, § 976.

existed in the ecclesiastical assemblies, and to some
extent in the States General, at a much earlier date.[1]
The use of the lot is, indeed, a survival from the Middle Ages, when it was a common method of selecting
officials.[2] The Bureaux meet separately and have three
functions. The first is that of making a preliminary
examination of the credentials of members of the Chamber, which are divided among them for the purpose.
The second is that of holding a preliminary discussion
on bills brought into the Chamber, before they are
referred to a committee; but as a matter of fact this
discussion is perfunctory, and is limited to finding out
in a general way what members of the Bureau favor
or oppose the bill.[3] The third and most important
function of the Bureaux is the election of committees,
for with rare exceptions all the committees of both
Chambers are selected in the same way. Each of the
Bureaux chooses one of its own members, and the persons so elected together constitute the committee. In
the case of the more important committees it is sometimes desirable to have a larger number of members,
and if so the Bureaux choose in like manner two or
even three members apiece, — the Chamber in each case

[1] Sciout, *Histoire de la Constitution Civile du Clergé*, p. 36. While
writing, a friend has pointed out to me that the States General which met
at Tours in 1484 was divided into six sections by provinces. See a journal of this body by Jehan Masselin, in the *Collection de Documents inédits
sur l'Histoire de France publiés par ordre du Roi*, Paris, 1835, pp. 66–73.

[2] The chief relic of the lot left in Anglo-Saxon institutions is, of course,
its use in the selection of the jury, — a survival which is due to the fact
already pointed out, that the English royal justice developed at an early
period.

[3] Dupriez, vol. ii. p. 404.

directing, by its rules or by special vote, the number of members to be elected. Thus the committee on the budget, which is the most important one of the year, consists of three members chosen by each of the Bureaux in the Chamber of Deputies, and contains, therefore, thirty-three members; while the corresponding committee in the Senate contains eighteen members, or two from each Bureau.

The committee on the budget and the one appointed to audit the accounts of the government are permanent, and remain unchanged for a year. A few of the others (those on local affairs, on petitions, on leave of absence, and on granting permission to members of parliament to introduce bills) serve for a month and then are chosen afresh. With these exceptions every measure is in theory referred to a special committee elected by the Bureaux for the purpose; but as there are certain to be in every session a number of bills that cover very much the same ground, a rigid application of this principle would result in inconsistent reports on the same matter by different committees, and would throw the work of the Chamber into utter confusion. A practice has, therefore, grown up of treating certain committees — such as those on the army, on labor, and on railroads — as virtually permanent, and referring to them all bills on their respective subjects.[1]

We have seen that with rare exceptions all committees, whether permanent, temporary, or special, are elected by the Bureaux, but these last, being created anew every month, acquire no corporate feeling, and hence have

[1] Dupriez, vol. ii. pp. 385-86.

no real leaders. Owing partly to this fact they do not choose freely, and the chief of the parliamentary groups meet and barter away the places on the important committees, which are thus cut and dried beforehand.[1] But whether the choice of committee-men is really made by the Bureaux or dictated by the chiefs of the groups, the main point to notice is that the system is entirely inconsistent with the parliamentary form of government. The cabinet cannot exert the same influence over an election conducted in this way that it could over one made by the Chamber in open session. In the latter case it might insist on the choice of a majority of the committee from among its own friends, and make of the matter a cabinet question; but it cannot treat the failure of several irresponsible sections of the Chamber to act in accordance with its wishes as an expression of want of confidence by the Chamber as a whole. The result is that the committees are not nominated by the cabinet, or necessarily in sympathy with it; and yet all measures, including those proposed by the government, are referred to them to revise as they think best. Now if the ministers are to be responsible for directing the work of the Chamber, they ought to have a policy of their own and stand or fall on that. They ought to be at liberty to determine their own course of action, and to present their measures to Parliament in a form that they entirely approve. But if a committee has power to amend government bills, the ministers must either assume the burden of trying to persuade the Chamber to reverse the amendments, with all the influence of the

[1] Cf. Simon, *Nos Hommes d'Etat*, pp. 41, 241.

committee against them; or they must take the risk of opposing the bill as reported, although they still approve of many of its features; or finally they must accept the bill as it stands, and become responsible for a measure with which they are not themselves fully satisfied. The committees in fact use their power without shrinking, and the annual budget, for example, has been compared to a tennis-ball sent backward and forward between the minister and the committee until a compromise can be reached.[1]

M. Dupriez, in his excellent work on the ministers in the principal countries of Europe and America, paints in very strong colors the evils of the French committee system. He points out how little influence the ministers have with the committees, who often regard them almost as the representatives of a hostile power in the state.[2] He shows that while the ministers have no right to be present at committee meetings, and are invited to attend only when they wish to express their views, the committees claim a right to examine the administrative offices, insist on seeing books and papers, and volunteer advice.[3] So little respect, indeed, do the committees pay to the opinions of the cabinet, and so freely do they amend its bills, that, as M. Dupriez sarcastically remarks, the government and the committee are never in perfect accord except when the former submits to the latter.[4] He says, moreover, that when a bill comes up for

[1] Simon, *Souviens toi du Deux Décembre*, p. 314.
[2] Vol. ii. pp. 406–7. [3] *Id.*, pp. 395, 405, 423–24, 438–39.
[4] *Id.*, pp. 405–6, 412.

debate the reporter of the committee is a rival who has great influence with the Chamber, while the deputies are inclined to regard the ministers with jealousy and defiance.[1] Nor do the woes of the cabinet end here, for its authority is reduced to so low a point that its bills are quite freely amended during the debate on the motion of individual deputies.[2]

Of all the committees, the most domineering and vexatious is that on the budget. This committee seems to take pride in criticising the estimates and making them over, both as regards income and expenditures, while each member exerts himself to add appropriations for the benefit of his own constituents, so that when the report is finally made the government can hardly recognize its own work.[3] In strong contrast with all this is Dupriez's description of the procedure on the budget in England.[4] There the authority of the ministers is expressly protected by a standing order of the House of Commons to the effect that no petition or motion for the expenditure of the public revenue shall be entertained except on the recommendation of the Crown; and in accordance with a firmly established practice proposals for national taxes originate only with the government. In regard to amendments of the budget, members of the House may move to diminish, but not to increase an appropriation, and as a matter of fact the budget is rarely amended by the House at all. The comparison of the English and French methods of dealing with the budget goes far to explain the differ-

[1] Dupriez, vol. ii., p. 411. [3] Id., pp. 425–26.
[2] Id., p. 412. [4] Id., vol. i. pp. 110–12.

ence in the position of the two cabinets. Such a state
of things as exists in France cannot fail to lessen the
authority and dignity of the ministers, and place them
at the mercy of the committees. It prevents them
from framing their own programme, and insisting that
the deputies shall accept or reject it as it stands;
and thus, instead of compelling the majority to act
solidly together under the leadership of the cabinet, it
allows any deputy to use his place on a committee as a
means of urging his own personal views. Hence it
tends to dislocate the majority and break it into sections, with policies more or less out of harmony with
each other. While, therefore, the French scheme of committees has good points, and some features that might
be very valuable under another form of government, it
is clearly incompatible with the parliamentary system.[1]

The habit of addressing interpellations to the ministers has a direct bearing on the stability of Interpella-
the cabinet and the subdivision of parties; tions.
for it cannot be repeated too often that these things
are inseparable. The existence of the ministry depends
on the support of the majority, and if that is compact
and harmonious, the ministry will be strong and
durable ; if not, it will be feeble and short-lived. The
converse is also true. The cohesive force that unites
the majority is loyalty to the cabinet and submission
to its guidance, but if the cabinets are weak, or are
constantly overthrown at short intervals, they cannot

[1] Lebon, *L'Allemagne*, p. 88, remarks that the Bureaux in the French
Chamber were intended to subdivide the factions, and accomplish this
only too well.

acquire the authority that is necessary to lead the majority and weld it into a single party. This is especially the case when the crises occur over matters which are not of vital consequence to the bulk of the followers of the government, and yet that is precisely the state of things that interpellations tend to create.

It is of the essence of parliamentary government that the majority should support the ministers so long, and only so long, as it approves of their course, and this means their course as a whole, in administration as well as in legislation ; for parliament, having the fate of the ministers in its hands, holds them responsible for all their acts, and has gradually extended its supervision over the whole field of government. Now a parliament can judge of the legislative policy of the cabinet by the bills it introduces, but it is not so easy to get the information necessary for a sound opinion on the efficiency of the administration. It is largely to satisfy this need that a practice has grown up in the House of Commons of asking the ministers questions, which may relate to any conceivable subject, and afford a means of putting the cabinet through a very searching examination. Of course the privilege is freely used to harass the government, but the answer is not followed by a general debate, or by a vote, except in the unusual case where a motion to adjourn is made for the purpose of bringing the matter under discussion.[1]

[1] The motion to adjourn is the only one that is in order, and since 1882 its use has been carefully limited. May, *Parl. Practice*, 10th ed. p. 240 *et seq.* In this form or some other a vote is occasionally taken on a single detail of administration. The most famous instances of late years have been the affair of Miss Cass in 1887, where the House of

A similar practice has been adopted in France, and questions are addressed to the ministers by members who really want information. But another kind of question has also developed, which is used not to get information, but to call the cabinet to account, and force the Chamber to pass judgment upon its conduct. This is the interpellation.[1] In form it is similar to the question, but the procedure in the two cases is quite different. A question can be addressed to a minister only with his consent, whereas the interpellation is a matter of right, which any deputy may exercise, without regard to the wishes of the cabinet. The time, moreover, when it shall be made is fixed by the Chamber itself, and except in matters relating to foreign affairs, the date cannot be set more than a month ahead. But by far the most important difference consists in the fact that the author of the question can alone reply to the minister, no further discussion being permitted, and no motion being in order; while the interpellation is followed both by a general debate and by motions. These are in the form of motions to

---

Commons expressed its disapproval of the government's refusal to make an inquiry by voting to adjourn, but where no member of the cabinet felt obliged to resign; and the defeat of Lord Rosebery's ministry in 1895. In the last case a motion was made to reduce the salary of the Secretary of State for War, in order to draw attention to the lack of a sufficient supply of ammunition, and the motion was carried; but there can be no doubt that the cabinet would not have resigned if its position had not already been hopeless.

In the House of Lords questions can always be debated. May, p. 206.

[1] For the rules and practice in the case of questions, see Poudra et Pierre, liv. vii. ch. iii., and Supp. 1879–80, § 1539. In the case of interpellations, *Id.*, liv. vii. ch. iv.

pass to the order of the day, and may be orders of the day pure and simple, as they are called, which contain no expression of opinion, or they may be what are termed orders of the day with a motive, such as " the Chamber, approving the declarations of the Government, passes to the order of the day." Several orders of this kind are often moved, and they are put to the vote in succession. The ministers select one of them (usually one proposed by their friends for the purpose), and declare that they will accept that. If it is rejected by the Chamber, or if a hostile order of the day is adopted, and the matter is thought to be of sufficient importance, the cabinet resigns. This is a very common way of upsetting a ministry, but it is one which puts the cabinet in a position of great disadvantage, for a government would be superhuman that never made mistakes, and yet here is a method by which any of its acts can be brought before the Chamber, and a vote forced on the question whether it made a mistake or not. Moreover, members of the opposition are given a chance to employ their ingenuity in framing orders of the day so as to catch the votes of those deputies who are in sympathy with the cabinet, but cannot approve of the act in question.[1] Now if adverse votes

[1] A very good example of the various shades of praise or blame that may be expressed by orders of the day can be found in the *Journal Officiel* for July 9, 1893. There had been a riot in Paris, which had not been suppressed without violence and even bloodshed. The police were accused of wanton brutality, and an interpellation on the subject was debated in the Chamber of Deputies on July 8. The order of the day quoted in the text, "The Chamber, approving the declarations of the government, passes to the order of the day," was adopted, but the following were also moved : —

in the Chamber are to be followed by the resignation of the cabinet and the formation of a new one, it is evident that to secure the proper stability and permanence in the ministry, such votes ought to be taken only on measures of really great importance, or on questions that involve the whole policy and conduct of the

"The Chamber, disapproving the acts of brutality of which the police have been guilty, requests the government to give to the police instructions and orders more conformable to the laws of justice and humanity."

" The Chamber, disapproving the proceedings of the police, passes to the order of the day."

" The Chamber, approving the declarations of the government, and persuaded that it will take measures to prevent the violence of the police officials, passes to the order of the day."

" The Chamber, censuring the policy of provocation and reaction on the part of the government, passes to the order of the day."

"The Chamber, hoping that the government will give a prompt and legitimate satisfaction to public opinion, passes to the order of the day."

"Considering that the government has acknowledged from the tribune that its policy has caused in Paris 'sad occurrences,' 'deeds that must certainly be regretted,' and 'some acts of brutality,' the Chamber takes notice of the admission of the President of the Council, demands that the exercise of power shall be inspired by the indefeasible sentiments of justice, of foresight, and of humanity, and passes to the order of the day."

" The Chamber, convinced that the government of the Republic ought to make the law respected and maintain order, approving the declarations of the government, passes to the order of the day."

" The Chamber, regretting the acts of violence on the part of the police, and taking notice of the declarations of the government, passes to the order of the day."

"The Chamber, approving the declaration whereby the government has announced its desire to put an end to the practices and habits of the police which have been pointed out, passes to the order of the day."

"The Chamber, convinced of the necessity of causing the laws to be respected by all citizens, passes to the order of the day."

In this case, by voting priority for the first of these motions and adopting it, the Chamber avoided the snares prepared for it by the ingenious wording of the others.

administration.   It is evident also that they ought not
to be taken hastily, or under excitement, but only after
the Chamber has deliberately made up its mind that it
disapproves of the cabinet, and that the country would
on the whole be benefited by a change of ministers.
The reverse of all this is true of the French system of
interpellations, and a cabinet which in the morning
sees no danger ahead, and enjoys the confidence of the
Chamber and the nation, may be upset before nightfall
by a vote provoked in a moment of excitement on a
matter of secondary importance.

The frequency with which interpellations are used to
upset the cabinet may be judged by the fact that out of
the twenty-one ministries that resigned in consequence
of a vote of the Chamber of Deputies during the
years 1879–1896, ten went to pieces on account of
orders of the day moved after an interpellation, or in
the course of debate.[1]   Several of these orders covered,
indeed, the general policy of the cabinet, but others —
like the one relating to the attendance of the employees
of the state railroads at a congress of labor unions,
which occasioned the resignation of Casimir-Perier's ministry in May, 1894 — had no such broad significance.
Moreover, the production of actual cabinet crises is by

[1] Cf. Haucour, *Gouvernements et ministères de la 111e république fran-
çaise (1870-1893)* ; Muel, *Gouvernements, ministères et constitutions de la
France depuis cent ans.*

Among the resignations brought about in this way, I have counted that
of Rouvier's cabinet in 1887, although this was caused not by the vote of
an order of the day, but by the refusal of the Chamber to postpone the
debate on an interpellation, and although the cabinet continued to hold
office for a few days pending the resignation of President Grévy.

no means the whole evil caused by interpellations. The enfeebling of the authority of the ministers by hostile votes about affairs on which they do not feel bound to stake their office is, perhaps, an even more serious matter, for no cabinet can retain the prestige that is necessary to lead the Chambers in a parliamentary government, if it is to be constantly censured and put in a minority even in questions of detail. The ministers are not obliged, it is true, to answer interpellations,[1] but unless some reason of state can be given for refusing, such as that an answer would prejudice diplomatic negotiations, a refusal would amount to a confession of error, or would indicate a desire to conceal the fact, and would weaken very much the position of the cabinet.

The large part that interpellations play in French politics is shown by the fact that they arouse more popular interest than the speeches on great measures;[2] and, indeed, the most valuable quality for a minister to possess is a ready tact and quick wit in answering them.[3]

The first two institutions referred to as not in harmony with parliamentary government — that is, the method of electing deputies and the system of committees in the Chambers — have real merit. Both tend to check the tyranny of party, and under a form of government where the existence of two great parties was not essential, they might be very valuable. But, except in a despotism, the interpellation followed by a motion expressing the judgment of the Chamber is a

---

[1] Poudra et Pierre, § 1555. [2] Simon, *Nos Hommes d'Etat*, p. 27.
[3] Simon, *Dieu, Patrie, Liberté*, p. 379.

purely vicious institution. It furnishes the politicians
with an admirable opportunity for a display of parliamentary fireworks; but it is hard to see how, under any
form of popular government, it could fail to be mis-
chievous, or serve any useful purpose that would not
be much better accomplished by a question followed by
no motion and no vote. The plausible suggestion has
been made that the administration, being free from
supervision by the courts of law, can be brought to
account for its acts only in this way; [1] but surely the
same result could be as well accomplished by the
simpler process of the question, and it is hard to see
any reason for imperiling the existence or the prestige
of the cabinet to rectify some matter of trifling consequence. The practice arose from the fact
that, owing to the immense power of the
executive in France, and the frequency with
which that power has been used despotically,
the legislature has acquired the habit of looking on the
cabinet officers as natural enemies, to be attacked and
harassed as much as possible. [2] But such a view, which

Jealousy
and distrust
of the minis-
ters on the
part of the
Chamber.

[1] See Vicomte d'Avenel, "La Réforme Administrative — La Justice,"
Revue des Deux Mondes, June 1, 1889, pp. 595–96.

[2] M. Dupriez, in the work already cited (vol. ii. p. 253 *et seq.*), has
explained the strength of this feeling by a most valuable study of the
history of the relations between the ministers and the legislature in
France. He points out that it existed at the outbreak of the Revolution,
for the *cahiers* or statements of grievances prepared by the meetings of
electors held to choose members of the States General in 1789 express a
widespread dislike and distrust of all ministers as such. He then shows
how the Constituent Assembly tried to curtail the power of the ministers,
and reduce their functions to a simple execution of its own orders. It is
unnecessary here to follow the subject in detail. It is enough to remark
that a large part of the political history of France since the Revolution

is defensible enough when the ministers are independent of the Parliament, becomes irrational when they are responsible to it, and bound to resign on an adverse vote.

Strange as it may seem, the development of interpellations has coincided very closely with that of parliamentary government;[1] and, in fact, the French regard the privilege as one of the main bulwarks of political liberty. It is this same feeling of antagonism to the government that has given rise to the overweening power of the committees in the Chamber, and their desire to usurp the functions of the ministers. The extent to which this feeling is carried by the Radicals is shown by the proposal made some years ago to divide the whole Chamber into a small number of permanent grand committees, such as existed in 1848, in order to bring the ministers even more completely under the control of the deputies; the ideal of the Extreme Radicals being the revolutionary convention, which drew all the powers of the state as directly and absolutely as possible into its own hands.[2] The less

is filled with struggles for power between the executive and the legislature, in which the former has twice won a complete victory, and deprived the representatives of the people of all influence in the state. Under these circumstances the suspicion and jealousy of the cabinet shown by Liberal statesmen is not surprising.

[1] The practice was first regularly established at the accession of Louis Philippe, the period when cabinets became thoroughly responsible to the Chamber ; and it was freely used during the Republic of 1848. After the *Coup d'Etat* it was, of course, abolished ; but toward the end of his reign Napoleon III., as a part of his concessions to the demand for parliamentary institutions, gradually restored the right of interpellation. Finally, under the present Republic the right has been used more frequently than ever before. See Poudra et Pierre, §§ 1544–49; Dupriez, vol. ii. pp. 305, 317–18.

[2] Cf. De la Berge, "Les Grands Comités Parlementaires," *Revue des Deux Mondes*, Dec. 1, 1889.

violent Republicans are, no doubt, very far from accept-ing any such ideal, but still they cannot shake out of their minds the spirit of hostility to the administration which has been nurtured by long periods of absolute rule. They fail to realize that when the ministry becomes responsible to the deputies, the relations be-tween the executive and the legislature are radically changed. The parliamentary system requires an entire harmony, a cordial sympathy, and a close coöperation between the ministers and the Chamber; and to the obligation on the part of the cabinet to resign when the majority withdraws its approval, there corresponds a duty on the part of the majority to support the min-isters heartily so long as they remain in office. Par-liamentary government, therefore, cannot be really successful in France until a spirit of mutual confidence between the cabinet and the Chamber replaces the jealousy and distrust that now prevail.

A comparison of the political history of France and England during corresponding years shows to what extent the French procedure interferes with discipline and disintegrates the parties. In England the Liberals came into power after the elections of 1892 with a small majority in the House of Commons; and, although the sup-porters of the government were far from harmonious, were, in fact, jealous of each other and interested in quite different measures, the perfection of the parlia-mentary machinery enabled the ministers to keep their followers together and maintain themselves in office for three years. In France, on the other hand, the

Comparison of the French Chamber of 1893 and the English Par-liament of 1892.

elections of 1893 produced a majority which, if not so large, was far more homogeneous; and indeed, if we compare the position of some of the outlying groups with that of certain sections of the English Liberal party, it is fair to say that the majority in France was both larger and more homogeneous. Yet within two years this majority suffered three cabinets which represented it to be overthrown on interpellations about matters of secondary importance, and finally became so thoroughly disorganized that it lost control of the situation altogether.

We have surveyed some of the causes of the condition of political parties in France. Let us now trace a few of its results. In the first place, the presence of the Reactionaries deprives cabinet crises of the significance they might otherwise possess. The defeat of the ministers does not ordinarily mean the advent to power of a different party, because there is no other party capable of forming a cabinet, — not the Reactionaries, for they are irreconcilable and hostile to the Republic, and of late years have been far too few in numbers; nor those Republicans who have helped the Right to turn out the ministers, because by themselves they do not constitute a majority of the Chamber. The new cabinet must, therefore, seek its support mainly in the ranks of the defeated minority, and hence is usually formed from very much the same material as its predecessor. In fact, a number of the old ministers have

Results of the condition of parties.

Owing to the presence of the reactionaries, a change of ministry does not mean a change of party.

generally kept their places, at most an attempt being made
to gain a little more support from the Right
or Left by giving one or two additional portfolios to the Moderates, Radicals, or Socialists.[1] When
a ministry falls, the parliamentary cards are shuffled, a
few that have become too unpopular or too prominent
are removed, and a new deal takes place. So true is this,
that out of the twenty-four ministries that succeeded
each other from the time President MacMahon appointed a Republican cabinet in 1877 until 1897, only
three contained none of the retiring ministers, the average proportion of members retained being about two
fifths.[2]

Now, the fact that the fall of the cabinet does not
involve a change of party has two important effects: by
removing the fear that a hostile opposition will come
to power, it destroys the chief motive for discipline
among the majority;[3] and by making the Chamber feel
that a change of ministers is not a matter of vital consequence, it encourages that body to turn them out with
rash indifference. The result is that the cabinets are
extremely short-lived; during the thirty-seven years between 1875 and 1912 — there were forty-five of them, so
that the average duration of a French cabinet has been a

[1] Lebon, *France as It Is*, p. 94.

[2] Cf. Haucour, *Gouv. et Min.;* Muel, *Gouv., Min. et Const.;* Dupriez,
vol. ii. pp. 338, 343. The three exceptions were the cabinets of Brisson
in 1885, Bourgeois in 1895, and Méline in 1896.

[3] This is very clearly pointed out by Dupriez, *Les Ministres*, vol. ii.
p. 390.

little less than ten months.[1]   The same fact explains, moreover, the persistence of the system of interpellations, for if a change of ministry does not imply a different programme, there is no self-evident impropriety in overthrowing a cabinet on a question that does not involve a radical condemnation of its policy.

The subdivision of the Republican party into separate groups has also an important bearing on the character of the ministry.   Instead of representing a united party, the cabinet must usually rely for support on a number of these groups, and the portfolios must be so distributed as to conciliate enough of them to form a majority of the Chamber.[2]   As a rule, therefore, the cabinet is in reality the result of a coalition, and suffers from the evils to which bodies of that kind are always subject.   The members tend to become rivals rather than comrades, and each of them is a little inclined to think less of the common interests of the cabinet than of his own future prospects when the combination breaks up.[3]   Such a government, moreover, is essentially weak, for it cannot afford to refuse the demands of any group whose defection may be fatal to

Owing to subdivisions of Republicans, the cabinet is a coalition, and therefore weak.

[1] I have not counted the reappointment of the Dupuy ministry on the election of Casimir-Perier to the presidency as the formation of a new cabinet.

[2] Only on two or three occasions has the cabinet been supported by a group which has contained by itself anything like a majority of the deputies.

[3] Cf. Dupriez, vol. ii. pp. 348–49.   Lebon, *France as It Is*, p. 85, speaks of the never-ending struggles for mastery within the cabinet.

its existence.[1] The ministers are not at the head of a
great party that is bound to follow their lead, and yet
they must secure the votes of the Chamber or they
cannot remain in office. Hence they must seek support
as best they may, and as they cannot rule the majority,
they are constrained to follow and flatter it;[2] or rather
they are forced to conciliate the various groups, and,
It must win   as the members of the groups themselves
votes by   are loosely held together, they must grant
granting
favors.   favors to the individual deputies in order to
secure their votes. This is not a new feature in French
politics. It is said that during the reign of Louis
Philippe, the government kept a regular account with
each deputy, showing his votes in the Chamber on one
side, and the favors he had been granted on the other,
so that he could expect no indulgence if the balance
were against him.[3] Nor has the cause of the evil
changed. It is the same under the Third Republic that
it was under the Monarchy of July, for in both cases
the lack of great national parties with definite programmes has made the satisfaction of local and personal
interests a necessity.

We are, unfortunately, only too familiar in this
Political use   country with the doctrine that to the victors
of offices   belong the spoils. In France we find the
same thing, although it is not acknowledged so openly,
and is disguised under the name of *épuration*, or the

[1] Cf. Dupriez, vol. ii. pp. 347-48, 434-35.

[2] Cf. Simon, *Nos Hommes d'Etat*, ch. vii. p. iii.

[3] Hello, *Du Régime Constitutionnel*, quoted by Minghetti, *I Partiti
Politici*, p. 101 ; and see G. Lowes Dickinson, *Revolution and Reaction in
Modern France*, pp. 118-20.

purification of the administration from the enemies of
the Republic.   The practice of turning political foes
out of office and substituting one's friends seems to
have begun during President MacMahon's contest with
the Chamber, when the Reactionary party dismissed a
large number of officials who had served under former
cabinets.[1]   After the Right had been overthrown in
1877, there arose a cry that the Republic ought not
to be administered by men who did not sympathize
with it, and would naturally throw their influence
against it ; but although the fear of danger to the form
of government was no doubt genuine at first, the cry
became before long a transparent excuse for a hunt
after office.[2]   In speaking of this subject, however, it
must be remembered that France is not divided into
two great parties which succeed each other in power,
and hence a wholesale change of public servants, such
as has often taken place after a presidential election in
the United States, does not occur.   The process is continuous, but slower and less thorough.   On and other
the other hand, the evil in France is by privileges.
no means limited to office-seeking, for owing to the
immense power vested in the government, the favors
which the deputies demand and exact as the price of
their votes extend over a vast field.   Nor do they show
any false modesty about making their desires known.

[1] See Channes, pp. 18–19, 231–32.

[2] See the remarkable little book by Edmond Scherer, *La Démocratie et
la France ;* Channes, *Nos Fautes (passim) ;* Simon, *Nos Hommes d'Etat,*
pp. 114–15, and ch. vi. ii. ; Dupriez, vol. ii. pp. 502–9 ; Lamy, *La République en 1883,* pp. 6–8, 22 ; and see a highly colored account by Hurlbert,
" The Outlook in France," *Fortnightly Rev.,* vol. 55, p. 347.

They do not hesitate to invade the executive offices, and meddle directly in the conduct of affairs.[1] Even the prefect, who has the principal charge of local administration, is not free from their interference. He is liable to lose his place if he offends the Republican deputies from his department, and is therefore obliged to pay court to them and follow their lead. In short, the prefect has become, to a great extent, the tool of these autocrats; and his dependence is increased by the fact that nowadays he does not usually remain in office long enough to acquire a thorough knowledge of the local wants, or to exercise a strong personal influence. I do not mean that he has become corrupt; far from it. The level of integrity among French officials appears to be extremely high, and though wedded to routine, their efficiency is great;[2] but the discretion in their hands is enormous, and in using it they must take care not to displease his Majesty the Deputy.[3]

Of course the deputies do not wield this immense influence to forward their own private ends alone.

Deputies obliged to curry favor with the local committees.

They are representatives, and must use their position for the benefit of the persons they represent. But whom do they represent? The people at large? No representative ever really does that. So far as he is actuated by purely conscientious motives he represents his own ideas of right, and for the rest he represents primarily the men who have

[1] Dupriez, vol. ii. pp. 435, 507–8 ; Channes, pp. 253–56 ; Lamy, pp. 21–26 ; Laffitte, *Le Suffrage Universel*, pp. 54–59.

[2] Simon, "Stability of the French Republic," *The Forum*, vol. 10, p. 383.

[3] Cf. Channes, Letter of Oct. 1, 1884 ; Laffitte, pp. 56–58 ; Dupriez, vol. ii. pp. 471–72, 506–9.

elected him, and to whom he must look for help and
votes in the next campaign.   In some countries this
means the party, and those classes that hang on the
skirts of the party and may be prevailed upon to fall
into line.   But in France there are no great organized
parties, and hence we must consider how candidates are
nominated there.   The government, at the present day,
does not put forward official candidates of its own, as
was commonly done during the Second Empire; [1] and,
indeed, it is not supposed to take an active part in
elections.   This last principle is not strictly observed,
for the administrative officials at times exert no little
influence in important campaigns, and the government
is said to have spent a good deal of money to defeat
Boulanger in 1889.   Still there is nothing resembling
the control of elections under Napoleon III., and especially there is no interference with the selection of
candidates, this matter being left to the spontaneous
movement of the voters themselves.   The usual method
of proceeding is as follows : a number of men in active
politics in a commune, or what we should call the wire-
pullers, form themselves into a self-elected committee,
the members usually belonging to liberal or semi-liberal
professions, and very commonly holding advanced views,
which are apt to go with political activity in France.
The committees or their representatives meet together
to form an assembly, which prepares the programme,
nominates the candidate, and proclaims him as the candidate of the party.[2]   These self-constituted committees,

[1] Simon, *Dieu, Patrie, Liberté*, p. 372.
[2] Simon, *Nos Hommes d'Etat*, pp. 17–25 ; Scherer, *La Démocratie et la*

therefore, have the nomination entirely in their own hands;[1] and, except in the larger cities, a candidate owes his position largely to local influence and personal interests.[2] Sometimes he has won prominence by a clever speech at a local meeting. Sometimes he has earned gratitude by services rendered in his profession, or otherwise.[3]

After the candidate is nominated, his first care is to issue his programme, and under the system of single electoral districts, each candidate, as has already been observed, has a separate programme, which expresses only his particular views. The active campaign is carried on by means of placards posted on walls and fences, which make a great show, but win few votes; and what is far more effective, by means of newspapers and the stump.[4] The stump, curiously enough, is used

France, pp. 22–24 ; Reinach, _La Politique Opportuniste_, 186–88 ; Laffitte, _op. cit._, pp. 64–69.

[1] Since the system of _scrutin de liste_ has been given up and the single electoral districts have been reëstablished, the matter is said to have become somewhat more simplified. It is stated that the nominating committees are now formed, at least in many cases, without any meeting of delegates from the communes ; and that their function lies not in the selection of a candidate, but rather in helping the candidate in whose behalf they have been organized, and acting as his sponsors. (See Alfred Naquet, "The French Electoral System," _North American Rev._, vol. 155, p. 466. But see Charles Benoist, "De l'Organization du Suffrage Universel," _Revue des Deux Mondes_, July 1, 1895, pp. 15–20.) However this may be, the close relations between the deputy and a small self-constituted clique of local politicians, which is the essential point in the French electoral system, remains very much the same.

[2] Simon, _Nos Hommes d'Etat_, pp. 24–25.

[3] Chaudordy, _La France en 1889_, p. 96.

[4] Alfred Naquet, "The French Electoral System," _North American Rev._, vol. 155, pp. 468–70.

very little except by the candidates themselves,[1] who
constantly speak at political rallies, of late years frequently holding joint debates.[2]　Far too often, unfortunately, they also truckle to the personal ambition of
individual voters by flattery and the promise of favors,
a course that deters some of the best men from political
life.[3]　The wire-pullers, indeed, are not over-anxious for
really strong characters, because they prefer men whom
they can control, and use for their own purposes.[4]　If
they want anything they exert a pressure on the deputy,
who in his turn brings a pressure to bear on the ministers; and hence it has been a common saying that
the electoral committees rule the deputies, and the
deputies rule the government.[5]

It is asserted that, since the re-introduction of single
electoral districts, the power of the committees has sen-
sibly diminished,[6] and, whether this be true or not, it is

[1] Theodore Stanton, supplement to the article of Alfred Naquet,
p. 473.

[2] Alfred Naquet, *Ib.*　The newspapers at election time are full of
accounts of these meetings for joint debate, called *Réunions publiques
contradictoires.*

[3] Cf. Scherer, *La Démocratie et la France,* pp. 24–25, 39.　Direct bribery
of voters, though not unknown, seems to be rare, but the complaint that
elections have been getting a good deal more expensive of late years is
general.　Naquet, *Ib.;* Reinach, pp. 189–90; Simon, *Dieu, Patrie, Liberté,*
p. 373; *Souviens toi du Deux Décembre,* p. 91.

[4] Channes, *Nos Fautes,* pp. 379–81; Laffitte, p. 69 *et seq.*

[5] Channes, pp. 238–39; and see Scherer, *La Démocratie et la France,*
p. 27; Simon, *Dieu, Patrie, Liberté,* p. 378.
For this reason one frequently hears it said that the deputies do not
see the real people, but only their own political dependents.　Channes,
p. 38; Simon, *Souviens toi du Deux Décembre,* pp. 165–66.

[6] Naquet, "The French Electoral System," *North American Rev.,* vol.
155, p. 466.　But see on the other side the article of Benoist in the
Revue des Deux Mondes, July 1, 1895, pp. 17–19.

certainly easy to exaggerate their influence, for the dep-

uty must always consider other people beside the wire-pullers. He must try to strengthen his general popularity throughout his district. He is, indeed, expected to look after the political business of his constituents, and is a regular channel for the presentation of grievances and the distribution of favors; one of the complaints most commonly heard in France being that the deputies represent local and personal interests rather than national ones. But even this does not end his responsibilities. The traditions of centralization which make all France look to Paris for guidance, and the habit of paternal government that makes men turn to the state for aid, have caused many people to regard the deputy as a kind of universal business agent for his district at the capital, and burden him with all sorts of private matters in addition to his heavy public duties. Sometimes this is carried to an extent that is positively ludicrous. Some years ago a couple of deputies gave an account at a public dinner of the letters they had received from their districts. Some constituents wanted their representative to go shopping for them; others asked him to consult a physician in their behalf; and more than one begged him to procure a wet nurse, hearing that this could be done better in Paris than in the provinces.[1] Is it to be wondered that the French deputy should bend under the weight of his responsibilities?

If I seem to have drawn a somewhat dark picture of the position of the deputy, I do not want to be under-

[1] This is quoted by Scherer in *La Démocratie et la France*, pp. 34–35.

stood as implying that all deputies are alike; that many of them are not men of high character, who will not yield to the temptation and pressure with which they are surrounded. My object is simply to describe a tendency; to point out a defect in the French political system, and to show clearly the characteristic evils which that defect cannot fail to develop. The famous scandals about the bribery of deputies in connection with the Panama Canal, with which the newspapers were filled for three months, have thrown a dismal light over public life in France, and, although at first the credulous Parisians no doubt exaggerated the extent of the corruption, still there was fire enough under the smoke to show what baleful influences haunt the corridors of the Palais Bourbon.

Before closing, let us consider for a moment the political prospects of the country. The generous enthusiasm that greeted the Republic at the outset has faded away, and even its most *Prospects of the Republic.* ardent advocates have found to their sorrow that it has not brought the promised millennium. Such a feeling of disappointment is not surprising. On the contrary, it might have been surely predicted, for in every form of government that has existed in France since the Revolution the period of enthusiasm has been followed by one of disenchantment, and to this latter stage the Republic has come in the natural course of events. Now this period may well be looked upon as crucial, because as yet no form of government in France has been able to live through it. After a political system has lasted about half a generation, the country has always become disgusted with it, torn it down, and set up another,—a course that has made any steady progress in public life impossible. The effect has, in fact, been very much like that which would be produced by a man who should constantly root out his crops before they came to maturity, and sow his field with new and different seed.

The reason for such a state of things is not hard to find. Since the Revolution every form of government in France has been the expression or outward sign of a definite set of political opinions. So close, indeed, has the connection been between the two, that it has been impossible for men to conceive of one without the other, and therefore a fundamental change of opinion has always involved a change in the form of government. Any one who studies the history of the nation will see that there has never been a change of party without a revolution. There has often been a shifting of control from one group to another of a slightly different coloring, but the real party in opposition has never come to power without an overturn of the whole political system. Under the Restoration, for example, the ministers were sometimes Moderate and sometimes extremely Reactionary, but were never taken from the ranks of the liberal opposition. Again, during the Monarchy of July the different groups of Liberals disputed fiercely for the mastery, but neither the Radicals nor the Reactionaries had the slightest chance of coming to power. If space permitted, this truth might be illustrated by taking up in succession each of the gov-

Hitherto no change of party has occurred without a revolution.

ernments that have flourished since the Revolution, but perhaps it is enough to refer to the only apparent exception that has occurred. While General MacMahon was President of the Third Republic, power was certainly transferred from the Reactionaries to the Republicans, but the circumstances of this case were very peculiar. The Republic had hardly got into working order, and the struggle of the Reactionaries may be looked upon as a final effort to prevent it from becoming firmly established. The French themselves have always considered the occurrence, not as a normal change of party, but as the frustration of an attempt at a *coup d'état* or counter-revolution. This case, therefore, from the fact that it has been generally regarded as exceptional, may fairly be treated as the kind of exception that tends to prove the rule. A revolution in France corresponds in many ways to a change of party in other countries, but with this grave disadvantage, that the new administration, instead of reforming the political institutions, destroys them altogether. Of course such a method puts gradual improvement out of the question, and before the nation can perfect her government she must learn that the remedy for defects is to be sought through the reform, not the overthrow, of the existing system.

One would suppose that under the Republic no such difficulty could arise, because a republic means the rule of the majority, and the majority is sure to be sometimes on one side and sometimes on the other. But this is not the view of most French Republicans, and especially of the Radicals. These men, recognizing

that, on account of a want of training in self-government, the people can be cajoled, or frightened, or
charmed, or tricked into the expression of the most contradictory opinions, refuse to admit that any vote not in
harmony with their own ideas can be a fair test of the
popular will, and assume for themselves the exclusive
privilege of declaring what the people really want.   As
M. Edmond Scherer has cleverly said : " Let us add
that the God (universal suffrage) has his priests, whose
authority has never been quite clear, but who know
his wishes, speak in his name, and, if resistance occurs,
confound it by an appeal to the oracle whose secrets
are confided to them alone." [1]   The Radicals, therefore,
cannot admit a possibility that the true majority can be
against them, and nothing irritates them so much as to
hear the other parties claim that the people are on
their own side.   It has been said that the Republic will
not be safe until it has been governed by the Conservatives,[2] and the remark has a special significance in this
connection : first, because, until the Conservatives come
to power, it will not be clear whether the Republic has
enough strength and elasticity to stand a change of
party without breaking down ; and second, because the
right of the majority to rule, which is the ultimate
basis of the consensus on which the Republic must
rest, will not be surely established until each party has
submitted peaceably to a popular verdict in favor of the
other.

[1] *La Démocratie et la France*, p. 18.
[2] " La République et les Conservateurs," *Revue des Deux Mondes*, March
1, 1890, pp. 120–21. This means, of course, the conservative elements
among the people, and not merely the conservative Republicans.

If the Republic proves lasting, the form of its institutions will no doubt be gradually modified, but, whatever changes take place, one thing is clear: the responsibility of the ministers to parliament must be retained. In a country like the United States, where power is split up by the federal system, where the authority in the hands of the executive is comparatively small, and, above all, where the belief in popular government and the attachment to individual liberty and the principles of the common law are ingrained in the race, there is no danger in intrusting the administration to a President who is independent of the legislature. But this would not be safe in France, because, owing to the centralization of the government and the immense power vested in the executive, such a President would be almost a dictator during his term of office; and the temptation to prolong his authority, from public no less than from selfish motives, would be tremendous. Nor, in view of the tendency of the mercantile classes, and even of the peasants, to crave a strong ruler, would it be difficult for him to do so, as Louis Napoleon proved long ago. A President is able to overthrow a popular assembly because the French have long been accustomed to personal government, and because an assembly is incapable of maintaining a stable majority; because, in short, the French know how to work personal but not representative government: and the danger will continue until parliamentary institutions are perfected, and their traditions by long habit have become firmly rooted. The French President cannot, therefore, be

Probable changes in French institutions.

independent, and the only feasible alternative is to surround him with ministers who are responsible to the Chamber of Deputies. But if the parliamentary system must be retained, it is important to remove the defects that it shows to-day, and especially is it necessary, on the one hand, to diminish the autocratic power of the administration, which offers a well-nigh irresistible temptation to both minister and deputy; and, on the other hand, to give the cabinet more stability, more dignity, and more authority; to free it from the yoke of the groups in the Chamber, and from dependence on local interest and personal appetite; to relieve it from the domination of irresponsible committees, and from the danger of defeat by haphazard majorities; to enable it to exert over its followers the discipline that is required for the formation of great, compact parties; to make it, in short, the real head of a majority in parliament and in the nation.

VOL. I.

ITALY

CHAPTER III.

ITALY: INSTITUTIONS.

The perfection of its organization and the excellence of its laws preserved the life of Rome long after its vital force had become exhausted; and when the Teutonic tribes had once broken through the shell of the western empire, they overran it almost without resistance. Europe sank into a state of barbarism, from which she recovered to find her political condition completely changed. Slowly, during the Middle Ages, the nations were forming, until at last Europe became divided into separate and permanent states, each with an independent government of its own. In two countries, however, — Italy and Germany, — this process of development was delayed by the existence of the Holy Roman Empire, which claimed an authority far greater than it was able to wield, and, while too weak to consolidate its vast dominions into a single state, was strong enough to hinder them from acquiring distinct and national governments. The condition of Italy was further complicated by the presence of the Pope; for although the Papacy was an immense civilizing force in mediæval Europe, yet the constant quarrels of the Pope and the Emperor, and the existence of the States of the Church, tended greatly to prevent the development

Causes that delayed the union of Italy.

of Italy as a nation. The country was broken into a multitude of jarring elements, and even Dante saw no hope of union and order save under the sway of a German emperor. The north of Italy was full of flourishing cities enriched by commérce and manufactures and resplendent with art, but constantly fighting with each other, and, except in the case of Venice, a prey to internal feuds that brought them at last under the control of autocratic rulers.[1] The south, on the other hand, fell under the dominion of a series of foreign monarchs, who were often despotic, and, by making the government seem an enemy of the governed, destroyed in great measure the legal and social organization of the people. For thirteen centuries — from the reign of Theodoric the Ostrogoth to the time of Napoleon — the greater part of Italy was never united under a single head, and in both of these cases the country was ruled by foreigners. Yet shortlived and unnatural as the Napoleonic Kingdom of Italy was, it had no small effect in kindling that longing for freedom and union which was destined to be fulfilled after many disappointments.

By the treaty of Vienna, in 1815, Italy was again carved into a number of principalities, most of them under the direct influence of Austria. Most of them, but not all, for in the northwestern corner of the peninsula, between the mountains and the sea, lay Piedmont, ruled by a prince of the house of Savoy, with the title of King

Sardinia takes the lead in Italy in the struggle for Italian independence.

---

[1] Genoa was torn with factions, and was at times, though not permanently, subject to Milan or to France.

of Sardinia.   During the great popular upheaval of
1848, Charles Albert, a king of this line, granted to
his people a charter called the Statuto, and
The Statuto. in that year and the following he waged war
with Austria for the liberation of Italy.   He was badly
beaten, but succeeded in attracting the attention of all
Italians, who now began to look on the King of
Sardinia as the possible saviour of the country.   After
his second defeat, at Novara, on March 23, 1849,
Charles Albert abdicated in favor of his son,
Accession of
Victor   Victor Emmanuel, who refused to repeal the
Emmanuel.   Statuto in spite of the offers and the threats
of Austria, — an act that won for him the confi-
dence of Italy and the title "Il Re Galantuomo," the
King Honest Man.   The reliance, indeed, which Victor
Emmanuel inspired was a great factor in the making of
Italy; and to this is due in large part the readiness
with which the Italian revolutionists accepted the mon-
archy, although contrary to their republican sentiments.
In fact, the chivalrous nature of the principal
Dramatic
character of actors makes the struggle for Italian unity
the struggle. more dramatic than any other event in modern
times.[1]   The chief characters are heroic, and stand out
with a vividness that impresses the imagination, and
gives to the whole history the charm of a romance.
Victor Emmanuel is the model constitutional king;
Cavour, the ideal of a cool, far-sighted statesman;
Garibaldi, the perfect chieftain in irregular war, dash-
ing, but rash and hot-headed; Mazzini, the typical

[1] Professor Dicey speaks of this, and draws a comparison between
Italian and Swiss politics, in a letter to *The Nation* of Nov. 18, 1886.

conspirator, ardent and fanatical; — all of them full of generosity and devotion. The enthusiasm which their characters inspired went far to soften the difficulties in their path, and to help the people to bear the sacrifices entailed by the national regeneration. Over against these men stands Pius IX., who began his career as a reformer, but, terrified by the march of the revolution, became at last the bigoted champion of reaction. The purity of his character and the subtle charm of his manner fitted him to play the part of the innocent victim in the great drama.

When Cavour first became prime minister of Victor Emmanuel in 1852, his plan was a confeder- *Cavour's plan of an Italian confederation.* ation of the Italian States under the Pope as nominal head, but practically under the lead of the King of Sardinia. Now, in order to make this plan a success, it was necessary to exclude the powerful and reactionary House of Habsburg from all influence in the peninsula, and with this object he induced Napoleon III. to declare war against Austria in 1859; but when the Emperor brought the war to a sudden end by a peace that required the cession of Lombardy alone, and left Venice still in the hands of the enemy, Cavour saw that so long as Austria retained a foothold in Italy, many of the principalities would remain subject to her control. He therefore changed his scheme, and aimed at a complete union *Changed to a plan for a united kingdom.* of Italy under the House of Savoy.[1] The whole country was ready to follow the lead

[1] Jacini, *I Conservatori e l' Evoluzione dei Partiti Politici in Italia*, p. 55 *et seq.*

of Victor Emmanuel, and, except for Venice and Rome, which were guarded by foreign troops, the march of events was rapid. The people of the northern States had already risen and expelled their rulers, and early in 1860 they declared for a union with Sardinia. Later in the same year Garibaldi landed at Marsala with a thousand men, roused the country, and quickly overran Sicily and Naples, which decided by popular vote to join the new kingdom, — a step that was soon followed by Umbria and the Marches. The rest of Italy was won more slowly. Venice was annexed in 1866, as a result of the war fought against Austria by Prussia and Italy; and Rome was not added until 1870, after the withdrawal of the French garrison and the fall of Napoleon III., who had sent it there to protect the Pope.

It is curious that Sardinia expanded into the King-
Government dom of Italy without any alteration of its
of the King-
dom of Italy. fundamental laws, for the Statuto, originally
The Statuto. granted by Charles Albert in 1848, remains the constitution of the nation to-day. It has never been formally amended, and contains, indeed, no provision for amendment. At first it was thought that any changes ought to be made by a constituent assembly, and in 1848 a law was passed to call one, although, on account of the disastrous results of the war, it never met. By degrees, however, an opinion gained ground that the political institutions of Italy, like those of England, could be modified by the ordinary process of legislation. This has actually been done, to a greater or less extent, on several occasions;

and now both jurists and statesmen are agreed that unlimited sovereign power resides in the King and Parliament.[1] The Statuto contains a bill of rights; but, except for the provision forbidding censorship of the press, and perhaps that protecting the right of holding meetings,[2] it was not designed to guard against oppression by the legislature, but only by the executive. The Statuto is, in fact, mainly occupied with the organization of the powers of state, and has gradually become overlaid with customs, which are now so strong that many Italian jurists consider custom itself a source of public law. They claim, for example, that the habit of selecting ministers who can command a majority in Parliament has become binding as part of the law of the land.[3]

Let us consider the powers of state in turn, beginning with the King and his ministers, then passing to the Parliament, then to the local government and the judicial system, and finally to the position of the Catholic church.

[1] Brusa, *Italien*, in Marquardsen's *Handbuch*, pp. 12–16, 181–82; Ruiz, "The Amendments to the Italian Constitution," *Ann. Amer. Acad. of Pol. Sci.*, Sept., 1895. It may be noted that the various contributions to Marquardsen's work are of very different value, and that Brusa's is one of the best. He remarks (p. 15) that, before changing any constitutional provision, it has been customary to consult the people by means of a general election, and that it is the universal opinion that Parliament has not power to undo the work of the popular votes by which the various provinces were annexed; in other words, that Parliament cannot break up the kingdom. It has been suggested that the courts can consider the constitutionality of a law which involves a forced construction of the Statuto, but this view has not prevailed. (Brusa, pp. 182, note 3, 229–30.)

[2] Arts. 28, 32.

[3] See Brusa, p. 19.

At the head of the nation is the King, whose crown
is declared hereditary, according to the principles of the Salic law; that is, it can be
inherited only by and through males.[1] It sounds like
a paradox to say that the King is a constitutional sovereign, but that the constitution
does not give a correct idea of his real functions, and yet this is true. By the Statuto, for example,
his sanction is necessary to the validity of laws passed
by the Parliament,[2] but in point of fact he never
refuses it.[3] Again, the constitution provides that
treaties which impose a burden on the finances or
change the territory shall require the assent of the
Chambers,[4] leaving the Crown free to conclude others
as it thinks best; but in practice all treaties, except
military conventions and alliances, are submitted to
Parliament for approval.[5] The King is further given
power to declare war, to appoint all officers, to make
decrees and ordinances, to create Senators, to dissolve
the Chamber of Deputies, and so forth;[6] but the
Statuto also provides that no act of the government
shall be valid unless countersigned by a minister; and
in fact all the powers of the King are exercised in his
name by the ministers, who are responsible to the
popular House.[7] He is, indeed, seldom present at

The King.

*Power
actually
exercised
by him.*

---

[1] Statuto, Art. 2.

[2] Statuto, Art. 7.

[3] Brusa, pp. 105, 153 ; cf. Dupriez, vol. i. pp. 281, 292–97.

[4] Statuto, Art. 5.

[5] Brusa, p. 106.

[6] Statuto, Arts. 5–9.

[7] Statuto, Art. 67 ; and see Brusa, p. 105.

cabinet meetings, and has little or no direct influence over current domestic politics,[1] although it is said that his personal opinion has a good deal of weight on the relations with foreign states.[2] When, however, a cabinet crisis occurs and the ministry resigns, the King has a great deal of latitude in the appointment of its successor; for the Chamber is not divided into two parties, one of which naturally comes into power when the other goes out, but, as in France, it is split up into a number of small groups, so that every ministry is based upon a coalition. The King can, therefore, send for almost any one he pleases and allow him to attempt to form a cabinet. It often happens, moreover, that the man selected feels that he cannot get the support of a majority in the existing Chamber, but, hoping for a favorable result from a new election, is willing to undertake to form a cabinet if allowed to dissolve Parliament. In such cases the King exercises his own discretion, and grants permission or not as he thinks best; for, contrary to the habit in France, dissolutions in Italy are by no means rare. Thus the Italian King, although strictly a constitutional monarch tied up in a parliamentary system, is not quite so powerless as the French President or the English King.

In the selection of his ministers the King is not limited by law to members of Parliament, but, if a man is appointed who is not a member of either House, he is obliged by custom to become a can-

The ministers.

---

[1] Brusa, p. 108. Dupriez, vol. i. p. 289, says that he presides only when peculiarly important matters are under discussion.

[2] Dupriez, vol. i. p. 296. This is a common opinion.

didate for the next vacant seat in the Chamber of
Deputies, unless he is created a Senator.[1]   As in other
parliamentary governments on the Continent, however,
the ministers and their under-secretaries have a right to
be present and speak in either Chamber, although they
can vote only in the one of which they happen to be
members.[2] The work of the Parliament is, indeed,
chiefly directed by them ; for, while individual members
have a right to introduce bills, the power is used only
for matters of small importance.[3] As a rule, each
minister has charge of a department of the administration ; but it is allowable, and was at one time not
uncommon, to appoint additional ministers without portfolios, whose duties consisted solely in helping to shape
the policy of the government, and defending it in the
Chambers.[4]

The Italian Parliament has two branches, — the Senate
                      and the Chamber of Deputies. The Senate is
The Senate.   composed of the princes of the royal family,[5]

[1] Brusa, p. 108; and the same thing is true of the parliamentary
under-secretaries. *Id.*, p. 196.

[2] Statuto, Art. 66 ; Law of Feb. 12, 1888, Art. 2.

[3] Brusa, p. 172. Dupriez (vol. i. p. 308) says that the ministers in
Italy have not so complete a monopoly of initiative as in other countries,
and that private members often propose measures with success. But in
saying this he must not be understood to deny that the laws enacted as
a result of private initiative are unimportant compared with the government measures, both as regards number and character.

[4] Brusa, p. 197. See, also, the lists of the different ministries published
in the Manual of the Deputies. This manual, by the way, is a most valuable production, for it contains the text of many important laws and a large
amount of interesting information. For the organization and functions of
the various departments, see Brusa, p. 200 *et seq.*

[5] Statuto, Art. 34.

and of members appointed by the King for life from certain categories of persons defined by the Statuto.[1] These are: bishops;[2] sundry high officials, civil, military, and judicial;[3] deputies who have served three terms, or six years;[4] men who have been for seven years members of the Royal Academy of Science; men who pay over three thousand lire (about six hundred dollars) in taxes;[5] and men deserving exceptional honor for service to the state. Owing to the extreme severity of the Senate in recognizing such desert, there are at present only two members from this last class; for the Senate itself has the strange privilege of deciding whether a person selected by the King belongs properly to one of these classes, and is qualified to be a Senator.[6] Except for money bills, which must be presented first to the Chamber of Deputies, the legislative powers of the two Houses are the same, but the Senate has also judicial functions. It can sit as a court to try ministers impeached by the Chamber of Deputies; to try cases of high treason and attempts on the safety of the state;[7]

Its composition and powers.

[1] Statuto, Art. 33. All the appointed members must be forty years old.

[2] Since the quarrel with the Pope in 1870 this class has not been available. Brusa, p. 119.

[3] Except in the case of the highest officials, persons of this class can be appointed only after a period of service which varies from three to seven years, according to the office they hold. In 1910 there were ninety-nine Senators from this class.

[4] Out of a total of about three hundred and eighty-three, there were in 1910 about one hundred and forty-seven Senators from this class.

[5] There were seventy-one Senators from this class also.

[6] Brusa, p. 119; and see the Statuto, Art. 60.

[7] Statuto, Art. 36.

and to try its own members, — the Italians, curiously enough, having copied in their Senate the antiquated privilege which entitles the English Peers to be tried for crime only by members of their own body.[1] As a matter of fact, the Senate has very little real power, and is obliged to yield to the will of the Lower House.[2] In 1878–80 it did, indeed, refuse to abolish the unpopular grist-tax for more than a year, but gave way before a newly elected Chamber of Deputies.[3] It would probably not venture even so far to-day, for the number of Senators is unlimited, and on several occasions a large batch of members has been created in order to change the party coloring of the body, — in 1890 as many as seventy-five having been appointed for this purpose at one time.[4] As in other countries where the parliamentary system exists, the cabinet is not responsible to the Upper House; and it is only occasionally, and as it were by accident, that a minister has resigned on account of an adverse vote in the Senate.[5]

The Chamber of Deputies consists of five hundred and eight members, elected on a limited franchise. By the earlier law, the suffrage was so restricted that less than two and a half per cent of the population were entitled to vote; but this

The Chamber of Deputies.

---

[1] Statuto, Art. 37.

[2] The changes made by the Senate in bills have usually a legal rather than a political importance. Dupriez, p. 313.

[3] Brusa, pp. 155–56. See Petruccelli della Gattina, *Storia d' Italia, 1860–1880*, pp. 420–21, 558–59.

[4] In 1886 forty-one were appointed together, and in 1892 forty-two. See the list of Senators with their dates, in the Manual of the Deputies for 1892, p. 806 *et seq.*, and p. 876.

[5] Brusa, p. 158, note 3.

was felt to be too small a proportion, and in 1882 it was increased by an act whose provisions are still in force.[1] By this statute a voter must be able *The franchise.* to read and write, and must have passed an examination on the subjects comprised in the course of compulsory education,[2] except that the examination is not required in the case of officials, professional men, graduates of colleges, and others who could, of course, pass it; nor in the case of men who have received a medal for military or civil service, or who pay a direct tax of nineteen lire and four fifths (about four dollars), or who pay rents of certain amounts. The change more than tripled the quantity of voters at once;[3] and, although these still include only a small part of the citizens, it is to be observed that with the spread of elementary education their number will gradually increase until the suffrage becomes substantially universal.[4]

At first the members were chosen each in a separate district, but after the times of enthusiasm for Italian unity were over, and the generous impulse that had

[1] Brusa, pp. 122–27. This law, with its amendments, recodified in 1895, may be found in full in the Manual of the Deputies for that year.

[2] Education is compulsory in Italy only between the ages of six and nine. Act of July 15, 1877, Art. 2.

[3] It raised the number from 627,838 to 2,049,461. Brusa, p. 127. When the law went into effect, the voters were not very unequally divided into those who passed the examination, those who paid the taxes, and the other excepted classes. *Id.*, p. 126, notes 1–2.

[4] In order to restrict the arbitrary influence of the government over elections, and to prevent the abuses which had been common before, a procedure for preparing the lists of voters and insuring the secrecy of the ballot was established by the same law (see Brusa, pp. 127–28, 130–32) ; and in this connection it is to be noticed that soldiers and sailors in active service (including subalterns and police officials) are not allowed to vote. Law of March 28, 1895, Art. 14.

stirred the country began to give way before the selfish
motives of every-day life, it was found that the deputies
failed to take broad views of national questions, and
were largely absorbed by personal and local interests.
It was found, in short, that they represented the nation
too little and their particular districts too much;[1] and it
was hoped that by increasing the size of the districts
they would be freed from the tyranny of local influence,
and enabled to form compact parties on national issues.[2]
With this object the Act of 1882 distributed the five
hundred and eight seats among one hundred and thirty-
five districts, which elected from two to five deputies
apiece;[3] and, in order to give some representation to
minorities, it was provided that in those districts which
elected five deputies no one should vote for more than
four candidates.[4]   The new system, called the *scrutinio
di lista*, did not produce the results that were expected
from it.   On the contrary, in Italy as in France, where
the same remedy was applied to the same evil, the
organization and power of the local wire-pullers grew
with the increase in the number of deputies elected in
a district, while the influence of the latter over the
ministers and the provincial officers was greater than
ever before.[5]   An Act of May 5, 1891, has therefore

[1] Brusa, p. 16.

[2] Minghetti, *I Partiti Politici*, p. 18 ; Petruccelli della Gattina, p. 504.

[3] Three districts elected two deputies, sixty-one elected three, thirty-
six elected four, and thirty-five elected five. Brusa, p. 129. See Arts.
44 and 45 of the Act of 1882, and the table of districts annexed thereto.

[4] Act of 1882, Art. 65.

[5] Brusa, *Ib.;* and see Turiello, *Governo e Governati in Italia*, 2d ed.;
Fatti, p. 326 ; *Proposte*, p. 171.

abolished the *scrutinio di lista* and reëstablished single electoral districts.[1]

In accordance with the general practice in Europe, the deputies are not required to be residents of their districts, the only important limitations on the choice of candidates being the requirement of the age of thirty years, and the provision excluding priests who have active duties, mayors and provincial counselors in their own districts, and all officials paid from the treasury of the state with the exception of ministers, under-secretaries, and a few others.[2] The deputies receive no pay for attendance, but are given free passes over the railroads,[3] and it is no doubt partly for this reason that the small attendance in the Chamber has long been a crying evil.

Qualification of the deputies.

The Chamber is elected for five years, but so far its life has always been cut short by a dissolution, and in fact the average length of term has been less than three years.[4] The budget and the contingent of recruits are adjusted by

The term of the Chamber.

---

[1] This law is printed in the Manual of the Deputies for 1892, in place of Arts. 44, 45, of the Act of 1882.

[2] Brusa, pp. 132–34 ; and see Acts of Dec., 1860 (Arts. 97, 98), July 3, 1875, May 13, 1877, July 5, 1882, March 28, 1895 (Arts. 81–89). There is a curious provision that only forty officials of all kinds (except ministers and under-secretaries), and among them not more than ten judges and ten professors, can be deputies at the same time, and if more are elected they are reduced to that number by lot.   Law of March 28, 1895, Art. 88.   On account of some scandals that occurred at one time it is further provided that no officers of companies subventioned by the state, and no government contractors, can sit in the Chamber.   Brusa, p. 134 ; law of March 28, 1895, Arts. 84–85.

[3] Brusa, pp. 159–60.

[4] *Id.*, p. 139.

annual laws, and there would naturally be a new session every year; but in order not to interrupt the work of Parliament, and especially the consideration of the budget, which is apt to be behindhand, a curious habit has grown up of prolonging the sessions, so that three recent Parliaments have had only a single session apiece, one lasting two and a half and another three and a half years, all of them unbroken save by occasional recesses.[1]

The Chamber of Deputies elects its own President The Presi-   and other officers, and the vote for President dent.   used to be an occasion for a trial of party strength, as in most other legislative bodies. Of late years, however, the English habit has prevailed of re-electing the same man without regard to party affiliations;[2] and this is the more striking because the President appoints the committees on rules and contested elections,[3] which have, of course, no little importance. The idea that the presiding officer ought to be strictly impartial is not the only valuable suggestion the Italians have derived from England, for they have inherited Cavour's admiration for British parliamentary procedure, and in general they attempt to follow it. Unfortunately they have not done so in all cases, for, as we shall see when we come to consider the actual working of the govern-

[1] Brusa, p. 139; and see the list of the sessions of the various Parliaments in the Manual of the Deputies.

[2] Brusa, pp. 140 and 156, note 2. Biancheri was President of the Chamber continuously from 1884 to 1892. Manual of the Deputies for 1892 (pp. 800–802). In that year he was dropped for party reasons, and in fact the practice of looking on the President as the representative of a party has unfortunately revived.

[3] Rules of the Chamber of Deputies, Art. 12.

ment, the system of committees and of interpellations or questions has been copied mainly from the French and not the English practice.

Such, briefly stated, are the position of the King and the composition of the Parliament; but although the King and his ministers on the one hand, and the Parliament on the other, are the great political forces whose interaction determines the character of the government, still it is impossible to appreciate the relations between the two, without some knowledge of the method of administration, the principles of local government, and the control exercised by the courts of law, because these matters have a direct bearing on the functions of the cabinet, and hence on the nature of the influence exerted upon it by the Parliament.

The administration both of national and local affairs, and to some extent the judicial system of Italy, are modeled on those of France, and they present the defects without all the advantages of the original. This is particularly *The administrative system of Italy copied from that of France.* true of the administrative system, where Italy has copied the centralization, but has been unable to acquire the traditions which give real solidity to the body of officials. At first sight it seems strange that Cavour and his successors, with their admiration for English institutions, should have turned to the French bureaucracy as a pattern; but there were several reasons for their course. In the first *Reasons for this.* place the Napoleonic rule had already made the Italians familiar with the French form of administration. A far stronger motive came from the fact that after Cavour gave up the idea of a confederation, and strove to create a united kingdom of Italy, it became important, in view of the possible interference of foreign powers, to consolidate the different provinces as completely and rapidly as possible. The Italian statesmen tried, therefore, to make the people homogeneous; to remove as far as possible all local differences; and to destroy all possibility of local opposition.[1] The country, moreover, was very backward, and a great work of regeneration had to be undertaken, especially in the south, where society was badly disintegrated and brigandage was rife. To accomplish this a highly centralized and autocratic system, in which the government could make itself quickly and decisively felt, was thought essential;[2] and it was believed, not without reason, that until the union was accomplished, and order had been established in Naples and Sicily, it was impossible to introduce general local self-government or universal liberty. The old territorial divisions were therefore swept away, and replaced by artificial districts devoid, of course, of real local life. A centralized form of administration was set up, and the government was given a highly arbitrary power to interfere with the freedom of the individual. Such a system might have worked very well in the hands of a wise dictator, but, as some of the Italian writers have themselves remarked, it was so entirely inconsistent with the parliamentary form of government that one of them was sure to spoil

---

[1] See Brusa, pp. 23, 337; Jacini, *I Conservatori,* p. 55 *et seq., Due Anni di Politica Italiana,* pp. 93-94.

[2] See Brusa, pp. 253-54.

the other, and experience has shown that both of them have suffered grievously from the combination.[1]

There is a marked contradiction in Italy between the theory and practice of government; for there is a strong ambition to be abreast of the times and a general belief in the principle of personal liberty; but the actual condition of the nation has made it impossible to live up to these standards. A striking example of the contrast between aspirations and results is furnished by the state of the criminal law, for capital punishment has been abolished, in spite of the fact that homicide is more common than in any other civilized country in Europe,[2] and yet criminal procedure is in such a condition that thousands of people have been arrested on suspicion, kept in prison sometimes for years, and finally released because there was not sufficient ground for trial.[3] Thus by her code Italy appears to be in advance of most other nations, but in her criminal practice she is really far behind them. The truth is that

Contrast in Italy between theory and practice of government.

---

[1] Cf. Jacini, *I Conservatori*, pp. 67–68 ; Minghetti, *I Partiti Politici*, p. 100 ; Pareto, " L'Italie Economique," *Revue des Deux Mondes*, Oct. 15, 1891 ; and see Bertolini, "I Pieni Poteri per le Riforme Organiche," *Nuova Antologia*, June 1, 1894.

[2] Turiello, *Fatti*, pp. 330–32.

[3] See Speyer, in *Unsere Zeit*, 1879, vol. i. p. 576. Petruccelli della Gattina says (*Storia d' Italia*, p. 258) that in 1876, 93,444 persons were arrested on suspicion and let off because there was no ground for trial. This, it is true, was eleven years before the code was finally enacted ; nevertheless it illustrates the contrast between ideals and practice in criminal matters, and in fact in that very year the abolition of the death penalty was voted by the Chamber of Deputies, but rejected by the Senate.

the successive governments, in view of the unsettled state of the country, have been afraid to place restraints on their own power, and weaken an authority thought necessary for the preservation of order. Of course the result has been a good deal of arbitrary officialism and disregard of the rights of the citizen,[1] but while this is a misfortune for the north of Italy, extraordinary and autocratic power has at times been indispensable in Sicily and the south.[2] The impossibility, indeed, of giving effect to the theories of liberty that are constantly proclaimed from every quarter was forcibly illustrated by the only serious attempt that has been made to do so. When Cairoli and Zanardelli became ministers in 1878 they tried to carry out their principles thoroughly. They permitted the constitutional right of public meeting to be freely exercised, and gave up the despotic practice of preventive arrest, trusting to the courts to punish offenders against the law; but brigandage increased so fast, and other disturbances became so alarming, that the cabinet was driven from office, and its policy was abandoned. Of late years Zanardelli has again held office, and has succeeded in improving the administrative and judicial system to some extent, but the progress of the reform has been extremely slow, and the arbitrary power of the government, although reduced, still conforms even in quiet times far more nearly to French than to Anglo-Saxon notions.

There are two matters in connection with the admin-

[1] Cf. Brusa, p. 183.
[2] Cf. Speyer, in *Unsere Zeit*, 1879, vol. i. p. 581.

istration that require special notice. One of them is
the power of the executive officials to make
ordinances. This is even more extensively
used than in France, and there are complaints

The ordinance power.

that it is sometimes carried so far as to render the provisions of a statute nugatory,[1] although the constitution
expressly declares that "the King makes the decrees
and regulations necessary for the execution of the
laws, without suspending their observance or dispensing
with them." [2]   The interpretation put upon this provision is in fact so broad that the government is practically
allowed to suspend the law subject to responsibility to
Parliament, and even to make temporary laws which
are to be submitted to Parliament later, — a power that
is used when a tariff bill is introduced, to prevent large
importations before the tariff goes into effect.[3]   The
Parliament has, moreover, a habit of delegating legislative power to the ministers in the most astonishing
way. In the case of the Italian criminal code, for
example, the final text was never submitted to the
Chambers at all, but after the subject had been sufficiently debated, the government was authorized to
make a complete draft of the code, and then to enact
it by royal decree, harmonizing it with itself and with
other statutes, and taking into account the views ex-

[1] Brusa, pp. 170–72.

[2] Statuto, Art. 6. The courts have power to refuse to apply an ordinance which exceeds the authority of the government, but, in practice, this is not an effective restraint. Brusa, pp. 171–72, 175, 187.

[3] Brusa, pp. 186–87. In 1891 the customs duties on several articles were increased by royal decree, which was subsequently ratified by Parliament.

pressed by the Chambers. The same was true of the electoral law of 1882, of the general laws on local government and on the Council of State, and of many other enactments.[1] It may be added that although the Statuto does not expressly provide for it, the ministers, prefects, syndics, and other officials are in the habit of making decrees on subjects of minor importance.[2] The preference indeed for administrative regulations, which the government can change at any time, over rigid statutes is deeply implanted in the Latin races, and seems to be especially marked in Italy.[3]

The other matter referred to as requiring special notice is the civil service. The host of offi-

The civil service and its use for political purposes.

cials, who are, unfortunately, too numerous and too poorly paid,[4] can be appointed or dismissed very much at the pleasure of the government, for although there are royal decrees regulating appointments and removals in many cases, they

---

[1] Brusa, pp. 175–76 ; Bertolini, "I Pieni Poteri," *Nuova Antologia,* June 1, 1894. Several laws of this kind may be found in the Manuals of the Deputies. They are issued in the form not of statutes, but of ordinances, and begin by reciting the legislative authority under which they are made. It is a curious fact that Italian statutes vary a great deal, sometimes containing only general principles, and leaving to the government the task of completing them by supplementary regulations, and sometimes going into minute details (Brusa, p. 171). Dupriez, who looks at the matter from a French standpoint, says (vol. i. p. 336) that in the struggle between the government and the Parliament over the limits of the ordinance power, the government has tried to extend its authority beyond measure, and the Parliament to dispute it even in the matter of organizing the administrative service.

[2] Brusa, pp. 188–90.

[3] Minghetti, pp. 293–94.

[4] Brusa, p. 260.

do not appear to furnish a satisfactory guarantee.[1] Here, then, is a great mass of spoils, in the distribution of which the politicians take an active part.[2] Such decrees, providing for competitive examinations for admission to the service, are indeed common; and in 1890 a statute,[3] affecting the officers in the department of public safety, was passed with provisions for such examinations, and for preventing removal without the consent of a standing commission. But civil service laws, like all others, depend for much of their effectiveness on the persons who execute them.[4]

Let us look for a moment at the local government.

[1] Dupriez, vol. i. pp. 337–40 ; Brusa, pp. 252–55. For the scope of these decrees, see p. 261 *et seq.*

[2] Brusa, pp. 152–53 ; and see Dupriez, vol. i. pp. 340–42.

[3] Law of Dec. 21, 1890.

[4] There are two bodies that exercise a considerable control over the government. One of these is the Council of State, which has, however, only an advisory power, except in matters of administrative justice, and in the case of provincial and communal officials whom it protects from arbitrary removal. On this subject see Brusa, p. 212 *et seq.* The laws of June 2, 1889, which regulate this body, may be found in the Manual of the Deputies for 1892, p. 357. The other is the Courts of Accounts (*Corte dei Conti*), whose members can be removed only with the consent of a commission composed of the Presidents and Vice-Presidents of both Chambers. It has a limited supervision over the collection of the revenue, and passes finally on pensions and on the accounts of officials, provinces, and communes. It also makes a yearly report to Parliament on the accounts of each ministry ; but its most extraordinary function consists in the fact that all decrees and orders which involve the payment of more than 2,000 lire must be submitted to it for registration, and if it thinks them contrary to the laws or regulations it can refuse to register them. It is, indeed, obliged to register them if the Council of Ministers insists upon it, but in that case they must be transmitted to the Presidents of the Chambers together with the opinion of the *Corte dei Conti.* Law of Aug. 14, 1862, Arts. 14, 18, 19 ; and see Brusa, pp. 219–24.

The Italian statesmen had at first a general belief in
Local government.
decentralization,[1] but the force of circumstances and a repugnance to the idea of federation were so strong that the old territorial divisions, which could alone have furnished a solid basis for a decentralized system, were abandoned, and the whole country was cut up into a series of brand-new districts. These are the provinces, the circondari, the mandamenti, and the communes,[2] of which the first and the last are the only ones of great importance. Until the Act of 1888, the powers conferred on the local bodies were extremely small, and even now they are far from extensive, for the whole system is copied from that of France, and, with some variations in detail, the organization and powers of the French local officers and councils have been followed very closely.[3] A general description of the local government would therefore consist very largely in a repetition of what has been already said in the first chapter on France; and hence it is only necessary to touch on a few salient points, begging the reader to remember how great a power and how large a share of political patronage this

[1] In 1868 the Chamber actually voted an order of the day in favor of decentralization. Petruccelli della Gattina, pp. 192–95.

[2] In the provinces of Mantua and Venice the division is somewhat different, but is being brought into accord with the general plan. Brusa, p. 339.

[3] For a description of the local government see Brusa, p. 337 *et seq.* The full text of the law on the subject was fixed by royal ordinance on Feb. 10, 1889, in accordance with the Act of Dec. 30, 1888. It was followed by an elaborate ordinance regulating its execution, and on July 7, 1889, and July 11, 1894, by acts amending the law. Manual of Deps., 1895, pp. 301–94.

system places in the hands of the central authorities.¹
At the head of each province, which corresponds to
the French department, is a prefect appointed by the
King, and directly subject to the Minister of the Interior. Like his French prototype, he is regarded as
a political officer, and uses his influence more or less
openly at elections.² The chief executive magistrate
of the commune is the syndic; who is chosen, like the
mayor in France, by the communal council from its own
members, if the commune has more than ten thousand
inhabitants or is the capital of a province or circondaro;
and in other cases is selected by the King from among
the members of the council.* As in France, both the
provinces and the communes possess elected councils. In
Italy they are chosen for six years, one half being renewed
every three years; but the suffrage for these bodies
was exceedingly restricted, until by the Act of 1888 it
was extended so as to be somewhat wider, especially as
applied to the peasants, than the suffrage for the election of deputies.³ The abuse of local machinery for

¹ In practice the administration appears to be, if anything, even more
centralized than in France, owing to the habit on the part of the officials
of referring everything to the central government. Jacini, *I Conservatori*, p. 130; Minghetti, *I Partiti Politici*, pp. 240–41.

² Brusa, pp. 225, 277. On the eve of the elections in 1892, forty-six
out of the sixty-nine prefects were dismissed or transferred to other
provinces, in order to help the government to carry the country.

* By a law of July 7, 1896, all the syndics are now elected.

³ The other communal and provincial bodies are the municipal giunta,
which is elected by the communal council, and has executive powers;
the provincial deputation, which occupies a similar position in the province, and is elected by the provincial council; the prefectoral council,
appointed by the central government to assist the prefect; and the provincial administrative giunta, partly appointed and partly elected, which

political purposes, and the results on the public life of the nation, will be discussed later; but it is proper to remark here that the resources of the local bodies are not adequate for the fulfillment of their duties, and this, combined with a love of municipal display, has been the cause of heavy debts, especially in the case of the larger cities, many of which have long been on the verge of bankruptcy.[1]

The judicial system.

There is one branch of the Italian government which has not been centralized, and that is the judicial system. The lower courts are, indeed, new creations, organized on a symmetrical plan very much resembling the French; but, in order apparently not to offend the bench and bar of the old principalities, the highest courts have been suffered to remain in the more important capitals, so that there are now five independent Courts of Cassation, those of Turin, Florence, Naples, Palermo, and Rome, each of which has final and supreme authority, within its own district, on all questions of ordinary civil law.[2] The Court of Cassation at Rome has, it is true, been given little by little exclusive jurisdiction over certain special matters;[3] but the ordinary civil

Its decentralization.

has a certain share in administrative justice, and whose approval is necessary for the validity of some of the most important acts of the local councils. For a list of these acts see the Local Government Law of Feb. 10, 1889, Arts. 142, 166–71, 173, and 223.

[1] See Brusa, pp. 365–67; Turiello, *Proposte*, pp. 56, 63–65.

[2] A Court of Cassation is a court of last resort, which considers only errors in law in the decisions of inferior tribunals.

[3] These are, conflicts of competence between different courts, or between the courts and the administration; the transfer of suits from one court to another; disciplinary matters; and writs of error in criminal

jurisdiction is still divided among the five Courts of Cassation, which bear the same relation to each other as the highest state courts in America.[1] There is no appeal from one to another, and no one of them feels bound to accept the decisions of the others, or to follow them as precedents. One cannot help thinking that this is an unfortunate condition, because there is nothing that tends more completely to consolidate a people, without crushing out local life, than a uniform administration of justice. Italy has, indeed, a series of codes enacted at various times from 1865 to 1889, and covering civil law, civil procedure, commercial law, criminal law, and criminal procedure; but a code alone will not produce uniformity, because there is still room for differences of interpretation, and in fact the Italian Courts of Cassation often disagree, and there is no tribunal empowered to harmonize their decisions.[2]

As we have already seen in the case of France, the decision of civil and criminal questions forms only a part of the administration of justice in continental Europe, on account of the distinction drawn between public and private law.[3] In order, therefore, to form a correct estimate of the position of

The courts and the officials.

cases, in complaints for violation of election laws, in civil suits against judges, and in questions of taxes and of church property.

[1] For the organization and jurisdiction of the courts, see Brusa, pp. 231–38.

[2] Cf. Speyer, in *Unsere Zeit*, 1879, vol. i. p. 576.

[3] Belgium presents an exception, for there the officials can be sued, and the acts of the government can be reviewed by the courts, as in an Anglo-Saxon country. Cf. Kerchove de Denterghem, *De la Responsabilité des Ministres dans le Droit Public Belge.* For Switzerland, see chap. xi. *infra.*

the courts, we must consider their relation to the government, and their power to determine the legality of the acts of public officers. In Italy the prefects, sub-prefects, syndics, and their subordinates still enjoy the so-called administrative protection, that is, they cannot be sued or prosecuted for their official conduct without the royal consent.[1] This privilege is generally unpopular, and will no doubt be abolished when the proposed bill on the tenure of office is passed. Meanwhile the benefit of it is claimed more and more frequently, although the permission to proceed appears to be usually granted.[2] But even when this protection has been taken away, the courts will not have as much authority as in England or America. The reader will remember that the officers of the French government formerly possessed a similar privilege, and were deprived of it after the fall of the Second Empire. He will remember also that the change made very little practical difference, because it was held that the ordinary courts had no power to pass on the legality of official acts, such questions being reserved exclusively for the administrative courts. The result of abolishing the privilege will not be precisely the same on the other side of the Alps, because the problem has been worked out on somewhat different lines, a curious attempt having been made to establish a compromise between the English and the French systems.

[1] Law of Feb. 10, 1889, Arts. 8, 139.

[2] Brusa, p. 282 ; Turiello, *Fatti*, pp. 210–11. The permission to prosecute is not necessary in the case of offenses against the election laws. Law of Feb. 10, 1889, Art. 100 *et seq.* ; Brusa, pp. 73, 130, note 1.

ADMINISTRATIVE LAW. 147

The subject of administrative law is, indeed, very confused in Italy, and a few years ago it was in a thoroughly unsatisfactory condition. *Adminis- trative law.* When the union was formed, several of the component states possessed administrative courts of their own ; but in order to produce uniformity, and also with a view of furnishing the rights of the citizen *Powers of the ordinary courts.* with a better guarantee, an act of March 20, 1865, abolished all these tribunals, and provided that the ordinary courts should have exclusive jurisdiction of all criminal prosecutions, and of all civil cases in which a civil or political right was involved, the Council of State being empowered to decide whether such a right was involved or not.[1] It was not clearly foreseen that this last provision would place in the hands of the government an effective means of tyranny;[2] but such proved to be the case, for the Council of State, composed, as it was at that time, of members who could be removed at pleasure,[3] showed little inclination in disputed cases to recognize that any private rights were involved, and, there being no administrative courts at all, the government had an absolutely free hand as soon as the jurisdiction of the ordinary courts was ousted.[4] The attempt to place the rights of the citizen

[1] *Legge sul Contenzioso Administrativo* (March 20, 1865). See, especially, Arts. 1, 2, 3, 13.

[2] Perhaps it would be more correct to say that it was not foreseen how this power would be used for party purposes. Minghetti, *I Partiti Politici*, p. 270 *et seq.*

[3] See *Legge sul Consiglio di Stato* of March 20, 1865, Art. 4.

[4] See Brusa, pp. 212–13, 247 ; Minghetti, *I Partiti Politici*, p. 147 *et seq.*

more fully under the protection of the ordinary courts than in France had resulted in freeing the officials more completely from all control; for, except when strong political motives come into play, arbitrary conduct on the part of the French officials is restrained by the administrative courts. This state of the law in Italy gave rise to bitter complaints, but it lasted until 1877, when the decision of conflicts, as they are called, or

Administrative courts. disputes about jurisdiction between the administration and the courts, was transferred to the Court of Cassation at Rome.[1] Still there was no system of administrative justice, and hence, however illegal, and however much in excess of the authority of the official who made it, a decree, ordinance, or other act might be, no redress could be obtained from any tribunal unless it could be shown that an actual legal right was violated.[2] This omission in the judicial system was finally supplied by the statutes of 1889 and 1890, which reorganized the Council of State, created a special section of it to act as an administrative court, and conferred an inferior administrative jurisdiction on the provincial giunta.[3] In order to give the council a considerable degree of independence, it was provided at the same time that the members, whose number is limited, should be retired only on account of sickness and removed only for breach of duty, and in each case only after hearing the opinion of the Council of State itself.[4]

[1] Law of March 31, 1877 (Manual of Deps. 1892, p. 374).

[2] Cf. Brusa, pp. 247–50.

[3] These acts, June 2, 1889, and May 1, 1890, are printed in the Manual for 1892, at pp. 357 and 377.

[4] Act of June 2, 1889, Art. 4.

The section which acts as an administrative court enjoys a still greater degree of protection; for it is composed of a president and eight other members selected from among the Councillors of State by the King, and of these eight not less than two nor more than four can be changed in any one year,[1] so that, although the body has not the permanence of a court of law, it is by no means a mere tool of the government. Except in purely political matters, and in certain questions relating to customs duties and conscription, it has power to decide whether the acts of the central or local officers are authorized by law, unless some special tribunal or the ordinary courts have jurisdiction.[2] In brief, therefore, the legality of official acts is determined in civil cases by the ordinary courts when a question of private right, and by the administrative courts when a question only of interest, is involved. The function of the ordinary courts in these cases is, however, strictly limited to the protection of the individual, and does not involve an authoritative declaration of the law, for it is expressly provided that the judgment must be confined to the case at bar, and in that alone is the administration bound by the decision.[3] This principle is deeply rooted in the jurisprudence of the nation, for the Statuto itself declares that the interpretation of the law in such a way as to be universally binding belongs exclusively to the legislative power.[4] The Italian, indeed, has a dread of judge-made law, which is really the most wholesome form of

[1] Act of June 2, 1889, Art. 8.   [2] *Id.*, Art. 24.
[3] Act of March 20, 1865, Art. 4.   [4] Statuto, Art. 73.

legislation, — a prejudice that certainly seems very strange when we consider what a large part of the law of the civilized world, and especially of the law of the Latin races, was developed by means of the edicts of the Roman prætors.

It will be observed that the Italian system of administrative law differs from that of every other nation. According to the English principle, the ordinary courts have jurisdiction in all cases, and the very idea of administrative law as a distinct branch of jurisprudence is unknown. In most of the continental countries, on the other hand, all matters involving the legality of official acts are reserved for a special class of courts, which have exclusive cognizance of those questions which constitute the domain of administrative law; but in Italy both classes of tribunals are called upon to decide the same questions, the ordinary courts being specially empowered to protect legal rights.

The Italian system of administrative law differs from all others.

As seen on the statute-book, the Italian judicial system appears to be very good. It seems to provide the individual with more ample remedies, and a better guarantee against arbitrary conduct on the part of the officials, than can be found in most of the countries of continental Europe. But in fact the judiciary is not strong enough to protect the citizen effectually. This is chiefly due, no doubt, to the absence of those deep-seated traditions that are necessary to give the magistrates a controlling authority over public opinion. It is due also to the existence of the five independent

The judicial system apparently strong, but really weak.

Courts of Cassation, which prevents any one court from having the power that might be acquired by a supreme national tribunal; and indeed it is self-evident that a decentralized judiciary can hardly be expected to restrain a centralized administration. Nor is the protection afforded to the bench satisfactory.) The constitution provides that judges, except in the lowest courts, shall be irremovable after three years of service,[1] and by statute they can be retired only on account of illness, and removed only for crime or neglect of duty, and in these cases only with the approval of the Court of Cassation at Rome. But a judge is not protected against a transfer from one judicial post to another of the same rank, and although by royal decree a commission annually appointed by the court at Rome must be consulted before such a transfer can be made, its advice is not binding on the government.[2] The judges are, therefore, by no means entirely independent of the executive, and complaints are often made that they are altogether too much under its control. It is impossible to say how far these complaints are justified,[3] but it is certain that

Insufficient protection of the judges.

---

[1] Statuto, Art. 69.

[2] Brusa, pp. 277–78. In 1878 this decree was repealed for a time, and one hundred and twenty-two transfers were made in six months. Minghetti, pp. 134–35.

[3] Writing in 1878, Jacini (*I Conservatori*, p. 29) said that, so far, the judiciary had resisted all party pressure, but since that time this does not seem to have been true. See Minghetti, *ubi supra ;* Turiello, *Fatti*, p. 316 ; *Proposte*, pp. 234–35 ; De Viti di Marco, " The Political Situation in Italy," *Nineteenth Cent.*, Oct., 1895 ; Pareto, " L'Italie Economique," *Revue des Deux Mondes*, Oct. 15, 1891, *Giornale dei Economisti*, March, 1895, p. 353 ; Ruiz, *Ann. Amer. Acad. of Pol. Sci.*, Sept., 1895, p. 54 ;

the judiciary either has not enough power, or does not feel sufficiently free, to protect individuals against an oppressive abuse of political power, especially in local matters.   This is true even in tranquil times, while the wholesale resort to martial law by the proclamation of the state of siege during the recent troubles in Sicily and at Carrara shows that the courts are unable to cope with disorder on any large scale.[1]

The judicial system has been dwelt upon here at what may seem an inordinate length because its condition is one of the most important factors in the present political condition of the kingdom.

There is one institution in Italy which is not strictly

The church.   a part of the government, but is so closely

The Italians   connected with it, and has so direct an influ-
almost
wholly   ence on politics, that it cannot be passed over.
Catholic.   This is the Catholic church.   Within the
last quarter of a century every country in central Europe has found itself confronted with the Catholic question, and has been obliged to grapple with it; but the matter has a peculiar importance in Italy.   Not because the Italian is fanatical.   On the contrary, his intense religious fervor seems to have burned itself out during the Middle Ages, and has left him com-

Wolffson, "Italian Secret Societies," *Contemp. Rev.*, May, 1891 ; Lord, "Italia non Fara da Se," *Nineteenth Cent.*, March, 1892.   The charge that the courts were subject to political influence was made by the Parliamentary committee on the bank scandals in December, 1894.

[1] Contrast with these events the Chicago riots of 1894, where not only the military authorities never superseded the judicial, but where the national troops were called into action solely by means of the United States courts.

paratively indifferent; yet he clings to the church with a tenacity that is out of proportion to his zeal.[1] This is due partly to the fact that he knows no other creed, and partly to his conservative nature, but chiefly, perhaps, to the fact that the ceremonies and rites of the Catholic faith, having been moulded for the most part by his own race, are closely fitted to his temperament, and therefore continue to attract him strongly, especially on the æsthetic side. The nation is almost wholly Catholic, and to-day, as in the past, the church in Italy is assailed, not by heretics, but by her own children.

Cavour proclaimed the doctrine of a free church in a free state; but although the church is more independent of the government than might have been expected, it is impossible to carry the principle out fully in a country *The doctrine of a free church in a free state.* where there is only one religious body, and where that body has always been intimately connected with public life. The church could not be independent of the state in Italy in the same sense that it is in America, and this fact has led some of the Italian advocates of the doctrine to misunderstand it completely. They complain, for example, that the actual relation between church and state is based on the idea that the church is a private association instead of a public institution, and lament that the state has surrendered too much its

---

[1] Sir Charles Dilke, in his *Present Position of European Politics* (pp. 261–62), quotes the saying that the Italians would be a nation of freethinkers if they had ever been known to think, and remarks that although the epigram is unfair, there is a certain measure of truth underlying it.

control over the education of priests, [1] — expressions which amount to a complaint that the church is too free. But, although the principle cannot be applied rigorously in Italy, it has been carried out to a considerable extent. The state has abandoned the right of nomination to ecclesiastical offices, which had existed in some of the former Italian principalities; and the bishops are no longer required to take an oath of allegiance to the King. [2] Moreover, the so-called *exequatur* and *placet*, that is, the requirement of permits from the government for the publication and execution of the acts of ecclesiastical authorities, have been given up. [3] The state has also renounced all control over the seminaries for priests in Rome, [4] and rarely interferes with those elsewhere; [5] and finally the church has been granted freedom of meeting, of publication, and of jurisdiction in spiritual matters. [6] Conversely, the acts of the ecclesiastical authorities have ceased to be privileged. They have no legal force if they are con-

[1] See, for example, Brusa, pp. 426–27, 429.

[2] Act of May 13, 1871, Tit. ii. Art. 15. It has been decided that in the case of the lower clergy the oath was not dispensed with wherever it had been required by earlier laws (Brusa, p. 428); and even the bishops are not entirely independent of the state, for the royal *exequatur* is still required for the enjoyment of their revenues (*Id.*, p. 437). At times these have actually been withheld, notably in 1877. Speyer, in *Unsere Zeit*, 1878, vol. ii. p. 604.

[3] Act of May 13, 1871, Tit. ii. Art. 16.

[4] *Id.*, Tit. i. Art. 13.

[5] Brusa, p. 438.

[6] *Id.*, Tit. ii. Arts. 14, 16, 17. Religious processions outside the churches may be forbidden by the local authorities, if they are liable to interfere with public order or public health. Law of June 30, 1889, Art. 8.

trary to law or violate private rights, and they are not exempt from the provisions of the criminal code.[1]

A thorny question for the new kingdom was involved in the position of the monastic orders, many of which still held great tracts of land, but had long outlived their usefulness and were felt to be an anachronism. The solution adopted, though almost a necessity, was drastic, and illustrates how far the theory of a free church in a free state was at this time from being a reality. The order of Jesuits was absolutely excluded from the kingdom;[2] and even in the case of the other bodies, which had not aroused such violent antipathy, the government determined, while sparing the existing members, to forbid the enrollment of any new recruits. By the statutes of 1866 and 1867, therefore, all these monastic institutions and most of the benefices without a cure of souls were suppressed, and their property transferred to the state to be employed for the support of religion; but a pension for life was reserved to the present possessors, who were also allowed to remain in their establishments.[3] Every traveler will remember the aged monks in white frocks who may still be seen wandering among the cloisters of the Val d' Ema, near Florence. These are the last representatives of a mighty order that once overshadowed Christendom, and

Treatment of the monastic orders;

[1] Act of May 13, 1871, Tit. ii. Art. 17. The Penal Code of 1888 specially punishes abuse of language by the clergy. Brusa, p. 61.

[2] Brusa, p. 56, note 4.

[3] Acts of July 7, 1866, and Aug. 15, 1867. See, also, Brusa, pp. 431–33. By an Act of 1873 these provisions were applied to Rome, but in a modified form. Brusa, *Ib.*

with the spirit of romance which Italy cannot shake off even if she would, they have been allowed to drop away one by one until the monastery becomes silent forever.

The convents were not the only great landowners in the church. Many of the higher secular clergy were also richly endowed. But there was a strong feeling that the soil of the country ought to be controlled by laymen, and that the larger ecclesiastical incomes ought to be reduced. This feeling found its expression in the same statutes of 1866 and 1867, by which all church lands, except those belonging to parishes, those used by bishops and other dignitaries, and buildings actually devoted to worship, were taken by the state and converted into perpetual five per cent. annuities;[1] while all ecclesiastical revenues, not of a parochial nature, were taxed thirty per cent., or in other words partially confiscated.[2]

and of the endowments of the secular clergy.

By far the most difficult question was presented by the papacy. The Holy See had ruled over a territory of considerable size extending across the peninsula from the Mediterranean to the Adriatic. It pretended to trace its rights from a grant made in the fourth century by the Emperor Constantine the Great to Pope Sylvester, and in fact

The position of the Pope.

[1] Act of July 7, 1866, Arts. 11–18.

[2] Act of Aug. 15, 1867, Art. 18. By the Act of July 7, 1866, Art. 31, the revenues of bishops exceeding 10,000 lire are taxed progressively for the benefit of the general fund for religion, the whole excess above 60,000 lire being so taken. But if, on the other hand, the income of a bishop falls below 6,000 lire, it is made up to that sum out of the general fund (Art. 19). Similar taxes for the benefit of the fund are imposed on other ecclesiastical revenues. In the Act of 1873, Rome was more gently treated. Brusa, pp. 432–33.

its dominion was as old and well founded as that of any monarch in Europe. It felt that the sovereignty over its own States — the so-called Temporal Power — was necessary for its independence, and that if the Pope lived in a city subject to another ruler he could not remain entirely free in spiritual matters. But the Italians felt no less strongly that their country would never be a complete nation until it included everything between the Alps and the sea, with Rome as its capital, and this feeling was fully shared by the Romans themselves.

The northern and eastern part of the Papal States was annexed to the new Kingdom of Italy *The Papal* at the same time as Naples and Sicily, that *States annexed by* is in 1860; but Rome and the country about *Italy.* it was protected by Napoleon III., whose power depended so much on the support of his ultramontane subjects that he could not safely desert the cause of the Pope. Italy chafed under his interference, and waited uneasily until the war with Prussia forced him to recall his troops. Then came the revolution that overturned his throne. An Italian army at once crossed the frontier of the Papal States, and entered Rome on September 20, 1870.

The problem before the government was a delicate one, because any appearance of an intention *The law of* *the Papal* to treat the Pope as an Italian subject would *Guarantees.* have excited the indignation of the whole Catholic world, and might have led to foreign complications, or even to an armed intervention in favor of the Temporal Power. The cabinet determined, therefore, that

a law fixing definitely the position and privileges of
the Holy See should be passed before the seat of
government was moved to Rome. Recognizing the
peculiar relations of the Pope to other States, the
ministers proposed to make this law one of international bearing, so that it would have an effect analogous to that of a treaty, but they yielded to the firm
opposition of the Left in the Chamber, and the act
was finally passed as a piece of domestic legislation.[1]
This is the celebrated Law of the Papal Guarantees,
which was enacted in May, 1871, and remains unchanged at the present day. Its object is to insure
the freedom of the Pope in the exercise of all his
spiritual functions, and for that purpose it surrounds
him with most of the privileges of sovereignty. His
person is declared sacred and inviolable; assaults or
public slander directed against him being punishable
like similar offenses against the King. Public officials
in the exercise of their duties are forbidden to enter
his palace or its grounds; and the same exemption
applies to the place of meeting of a Conclave or Œcu-
menic Council. Searching any papal offices that have
solely spiritual functions, or confiscating papers there-
from, is prohibited, and it is provided that priests
shall not be punished or questioned for publishing,
in the course of their duties, the acts of the spiritual
authority of the Holy See. The Pope is accorded the
honors of a sovereign prince, and persons accredited
to him enjoy all the immunities of diplomatic agents.
He is guaranteed free intercourse with the bishops,

[1] Petruccelli della Gattina, *Storia d' Italia*, pp. 93–94.

and indeed with the whole Catholic world, messages sent in his name being placed on the same footing as those of foreign governments. Moreover he is granted a perpetual annuity of over six hundred thousand dollars, which is entered in the great book of state debts, and is free from all tax. This grant he has always refused to accept, and every year it is returned to the treasury. Finally he is left in absolute possession of the palaces of the Vatican, the Lateran, and Castel Gandolfo, with all their buildings, gardens, and lands, free of taxes.[1]

It will be observed that this law, — which appears, by the way, to have been faithfully carried out by the Italian government, — assures to the Pope absolute freedom in the exercise of his functions as head of the Catholic church, and guards him against all personal disrespect. Nevertheless neither Pius IX. nor his successor Leo XIII. has been willing to accept it; and indeed they could not have done so without acknowledging the authority of the government by which it was enacted, and this they have never been willing to do. They have not ceased for a moment to protest against the destruction of the Temporal Power; in fact, they have avoided everything that could possibly be construed as a recognition of the Kingdom of Italy. The Pope has affected to consider himself a prisoner, and since the

Refusal of the Pope to accept the situation.

[1] This is the law of May 13, 1871, several sections of which have already been cited. There is a criticism of the legal situation of the Holy See from a papal standpoint by Comte Rostworowski, entitled "La Situation Internationale du Saint-Siège," in the *Ann. de l'Ecole Libre des Sciences Politiques,* 1892, p. 102.

the royal cannon opened a breach in the Roman walls at the Porta Pia has he placed his foot outside the grounds of the Vatican.[1] He has even refused to allow the clerical party to vote for deputies to Parliament, on the ground that this would involve a tacit acknowledgment of the legality of the existing government; and thus a large portion of the Italian people takes no part in national politics, although the same men vote freely and sometimes win victories at municipal elections.[2] Such a condition of things is very unfortunate, for it tends to create a hostility between religion and patriotism, and makes it very hard for a man to be faithful both to his church and his country. If the Italians had any liking for other sects, these would no doubt increase rapidly; but as religion and Catholicism are synonymous terms in Italy, the antagonism between church and state merely stimulates skepticism and indifference.

It is not easy to see how the papal question will finally be solved. Pope Leo XIII was a man of great tact, and with marvelous dexterity he changed the policy of the Vatican so as to bring it into harmony with the nineteenth century. He made a peace with Bismarck by which the Iron Chancellor virtually acknowledged defeat; and by his conciliatory tone towards the French Republic he made fair headway in checking the Radicals in France with their hatred of the church. Yet even Leo XIII was unable to come to terms with Italy. One thing is clear. Italy will

Solution of the papal question difficult for the Vatican.

[1] Until 1888 he did not even appear in St. Peter's.
[2] In 1905 an encyclical of Pius X somewhat relaxed the prohibition.

never give up Rome, nor is there the slightest prob-
ability that any foreign country will try to force
her to do so; and, indeed, it is said that even in the
Vatican the restoration of the Temporal Power is
considered hopeless.[1] To the outside observer it
hardly appears desirable in the interest of the papacy
itself, because with the loss of its secular functions, the
Holy See has gained enormously in ecclesiastical
authority. This is not an accident, for the destruction of the Temporal Power is one step in the long
movement for the separation of church and state,
which during the last hundred years has been breaking the local and national ties of the clergy in the
different countries, and has thus made the Catholic
church more cosmopolitan, more centralized, and more
dependent on its spiritual head. Such, however, is
not the view of many ardent Catholics, who are so
dissatisfied with the present situation that a departure
of the Pope from Rome has often been suggested; but
although on more than one occasion a removal has
been said to be imminent, it is in the highest degree

---

[1] In an answer (" Italy, France, and the Papacy," *Contemp. Rev.*, Aug.,
1891) to an article entitled "The Savoy Dynasty, the Pope, and the Republic," by an anonymous writer (*Contemp. Rev.*, Apr., 1891), Crispi
speaks of the possibility of a French intervention in favor of the Temporal Power as a real danger. One cannot help feeling that this must
have been said rather for its effect than from conviction. In a previous
answer to the same article ("Italy and France," *Contemp. Rev.*, June,
1891), Crispi makes the interesting statement that even in Rome only
the highest church dignitaries want the Temporal Power, while over the
rest of Italy the clergy never were papal, and are not so now. In a
later number of the same *Review* the Triple Alliance and the papal
question are further discussed by Emile de Laveleye (" The Foreign
Policy of Italy," *Contemp. Rev.*, Feb., 1892.)

unlikely, for the Holy See could not get from any other state in whose territory it might settle terms more favorable than those accorded by the Law of the Papal Guarantees, and even if it should accept a grant of complete sovereignty over some island or small tract of land, the loss in prestige from the change of residence would be incalculable. The veneration of the past still clings to Rome, and although the splendor of the Vatican is gone, the Pope bereft of his Temporal Power wields a greater spiritual influence than he has had for centuries.

GERMANY

CHAPTER IV.

GERMANY: THE STRUCTURE OF THE EMPIRE.

CHERBULIEZ has remarked that most countries which
have grown in size have started with a compact territory and increased it by absorbing
the adjacent lands, but that Prussia began
with her frontiers and afterwards filled in
between them. The statement is almost literally true,
for early in the seventeenth century the Electors of
Brandenburg, who were the ancestors of the Kings of
Prussia, acquired the large Duchy of Prussia on the
Baltic and the Duchy of Cleves on the Rhine, possessions which form to-day very nearly the extreme limits
of the Prussian monarchy on the east and west. At
that time these duchies did not touch the Electors'
other territories, and in fact until less than thirty years
ago several States were so wedged in among the Prussian dominions as to cut the kingdom quite in two.
Nor was this the case with Prussia alone. The whole
map of Germany as it stood in the last century was a
mass of patches of different color mingled together in
bewildering confusion. Not only were some of the principalities inconceivably small, but they often consisted in
part of outlying districts at a distance from one another,
and entirely surrounded by the estates of some other
potentate. The cause of such a state of things is to be

Subdivision of Germany under the Holy Roman Empire.

found in the excessive development of the feudal system, which treated sovereignty as a private right of the ruler, so that princes dealt with their fiefs very much as men do with their lands to-day. They acquired them freely in all directions by inheritance, by marriage, and even by purchase, and, what was worse, at their death they divided them as they pleased among their sons. Still another source of confusion was presented by the bishops and other high church dignitaries, who held large estates which they ruled as temporal sovereigns. The result was that Germany was divided in a most fantastic way among several hundred princes, who owed, it is true, a shadowy allegiance to the Emperor as head of the Holy Roman Empire, but for all practical purposes were virtually independent.

Almost alone among the German States Prussia was steadily gaining in size and power. Her growth may be traced primarily to the *Constitutio Achillea* of 1473, which forbade the splitting up of the monarchy among the sons of the Electors, and thus kept all their dominions together; but it was due chiefly to the thrift, the energy, and the sagacity of the rulers of the House of Hohenzollern. At the close of the thirty years' war, in 1648, the Great Elector obtained possessions which made his domains larger than those of any other German State except Austria, and in the next century the annexations of Frederic the Great more than doubled the population of his kingdom. The growth of Prussia was suddenly checked by an event that tended ultimately to hasten its development. This was the outbreak of

The growth of Prussia.

Checked for a time, but in the end helped by Napoleon.

the French Revolution and the career of Bonaparte. When a series of victories had laid Germany at his feet, Napoleon suppressed a large number of petty principalities including all the ecclesiastical ones, and combined the smaller States that remained into the Confederation of the Rhine. He also deprived Prussia of half her territory, thinking by these means to reduce her to impotence, and create in the heart of Germany a body that would always be devoted to the cause of France. But in fact the petty principalities had been too small to act separately or to combine effectively, and too independent to be made serviceable by any sovereign; and by suppressing them Napoleon had given the Germans some little capacity for organization, which was used against him as soon as the tide turned.[1]

After his overthrow Germany was reorganized by the treaty of Vienna, and the States, which now numbered only thirty-nine, were formed into a loose confederation. This was not properly a federal union, but rather a perpetual international alliance, the States remaining separate and independent, except for matters affecting the external and internal safety of Germany. The only organ of the Confederation was a Diet composed of the diplomatic agents of the different States, who acted like ambassadors, and voted in accordance with the instructions they received from their respective governments.

The Germanic Confederation and the Diet.

[1] This is very well stated by Colonel Malleson in his *Refounding of the German Empire*, pp. 4–6. Napoleon prophesied that within fifty years all Europe would be either Republican or Cossack. One of the chief causes of the failure of this prediction has been the creation of a united Germany, which Napoleon himself unwittingly helped to bring about.

It had power to declare war and make peace, to organize the federal army, to enact laws for the purpose of applying the constitution, and to decide disputes between the States; but it had no administrative officers under its command, the federal laws being executed entirely by the officials of the States.   Hence the only means of getting its orders carried out in case a State refused to obey them was by the process known as federal execution, which meant that the Diet called on one or more members of the Confederation to attack the recalcitrant State, and by invading its territories to compel submission.   The procedure in the Diet was a complicated one.   For ordinary matters it acted by sections called *curiæ*, when the eleven largest States had one vote apiece, the other twenty-eight being combined into six groups each of which had a single vote.   For constitutional questions, on the other hand, and those relating to peace and war, the Diet proceeded *in plenum*, and in that case each of the smaller States had one vote, while the fourteen largest had two, three, or four votes apiece.[1]   This distribution of votes was by no means in proportion to population, for the largest States were much more than four times as big as the smallest, but it was a distinct recognition of an inequality of rights on the part of the States, and as such it still retains an especial importance because the arrangement of the votes in the *plenum* has continued almost unchanged in one of the chief organs of the Empire to-day.   It must not be supposed,

[1] Six of the States had four votes, five had three, three had two, and twenty-five had one.

however, that the influence of the States in the Diet was determined by the number of their votes, for Austria, which had a permanent right to the presidency of the Assembly, and Prussia, which had a permanent right to the vice-presidency, exercised in fact a controlling authority. When these two great powers agreed they had their own way; when they disagreed, which often happened, the opinion of Austria usually prevailed.

The wars of Napoleon did a great deal more for Germany than to suppress petty principalities and give rise to a clumsy confederation. They awakened a sentiment of German nationality. At first this was only a sentiment, and for a long period it had no practical results. It was especially strong among the Liberals, and grew stronger as time went on; but under the reaction that followed the overthrow of Napoleon, the Liberals had little influence, until the convulsions of 1848 and 1849 brought them to the front. At this time they tried hard to bring about a national union of Germany, but they were sadly hampered by their theoretical views and their want of political experience. Their aim was a German state constructed on an ideal model, and they lacked the quality which is essential to real statesmanship, — the power to distinguish the elements in the existing order of things which have a solid basis, to seize upon these, and adapt them to the end in view. Hence their efforts expended themselves in declamation and academic discussion, and came to nothing. In May, 1848, they succeeded in bringing together at

Failure of the Liberal attempt to unite Germany in 1848–49.

Frankfort a National German Parliament elected by universal suffrage, and if this body had proposed quickly any rational plan for a union of Germany, the chances of its adoption would have been very good, for every government in the country had been forced to give way before the fierce onslaught of the Liberal movement. But unfortunately more than four months of precious time were consumed in debating the primary rights of the citizen, and when these were finally disposed of the tide was beginning to ebb. At last, in March, 1849, a constitution was agreed upon, and the imperial crown was tendered to the King of Prussia; but the offer came too late. Had it been made in the preceding summer it might have been accepted, but now the revolution had spent its force. Austria, at first paralyzed by insurrection, had now recovered from the shock, was rapidly putting down her rebellious subjects, and under the able leadership of Prince Schwartzenberg was determined to prevent any reorganization of Germany which would diminish her influence. After a feeble struggle Prussia yielded to her more determined rival, the revolutionary movement came to an end, and the old Confederation was restored.

Again a period of reaction set in, which lasted about ten years, when Germany was thrilled by the events in Italy, and the Liberals again became powerful. Whether they would have avoided their former mistakes and succeeded better it is impossible to say, for just at this time there appeared upon the scene a man who was destined to stamp his

Bismarck.

will on Germany, and change the whole face of European politics. That man was von Bismarck. He belonged to the lesser Prussian nobility, which is the most conservative class in the race; but he was of far too large a calibre to be bound down by traditional prejudices; and indeed he had already formed very decided opinions of his own on the subject of German unity. He had served as a representative of Prussia at the Diet, and had learned that a German nation was impossible so long as the two great powers — Austria and Prussia — were contending for a mastery. He saw that the first step must be the forcible expulsion of Austria from all share in German politics, and he believed that union could never be brought about by argument, that the Germans could not be persuaded, but must be compelled to unite, that the work must be done, as he expressed it, by blood and iron.

An important advance towards closer relations between the States had, indeed, been made long ago by the creation of the *Zollverein* or customs union. This had been founded by Prussia in the early part of the century, and had gradually been extended until it included almost all the German States, except Austria, which had been jealously excluded by the Prussian statesmen; but valuable as the Zollverein was in teaching the people their common interests, Bismarck was no doubt right in thinking that no further progress could be expected without the use of force. Now it was precisely on this point that his methods differed from those of the Liberals, for war formed no part of their programme, and for that very reason they were unable to understand his policy. In 1859 they had obtained a majority in the lower house of the Prussian Parliament, and The constitutional conflict. had very soon become involved in a quarrel with King William over the reorganization of the army, on which he had set his heart.[1] In 1862 the King turned to Bismarck and made him the President of the Council. Bismarck submitted to the chamber a budget containing the appropriations for the military changes, and when the chamber refused to pass it he withdrew it, and governed without any budget at all. This he was enabled to do, because the taxes were collected under standing laws which required no reënactment, and in fact could not be changed without the consent of the crown; and because a doctrine was developed that in case the King and the two houses were unable to agree upon appropriations, the King was entitled to make all those expenditures which were necessary in order to carry on the government in accordance with the laws regulating the various branches of the administration. The Liberals were furious at this budget-less rule, but Bismarck proceeded in spite of them. He persuaded Austria to join Prussia in wresting the duchies of Schleswig and Holstein from Denmark in 1864, and then contrived to quarrel with her about the disposition to be made of them. The majority in the German Diet sided with Austria, and ordered the

---

[1] William became Regent on Oct. 7, 1858, and on the death of his brother Frederick William IV., on January 2, 1861, he became King.

troops of the Confederation mobilized against Prussia.

The war of 1866. Then followed the war of 1866, and the crushing defeat of Austria and the smaller German States that took her part.

Prussian annexations and the North German Confederation. Bismarck had originally intended to compel all the States except Austria to form a federal union, but the intervention of Napoleon III forced him to abandon the plan, and limit the Confederation to the country north of the river Main.[1] He therefore determined as a compensation to increase the direct strength of Prussia by annexing the States that had fought against her.[2] Hanover, Electoral Hesse,[3] Nassau, and Frankfort, besides Schleswig-Holstein, were accordingly incorporated in Prussia, while with the other States north of the Main a new federal union was formed under the name of the North German Confederation.[4] This had for its president the Prussian King; and for its legislature two chambers, — one the Reichstag, a popular assembly elected by universal suffrage, and the other the Bundesrath, or federal council, which was copied from the old

---

[1] Luxemburg and Limburg, which belonged to Holland, had been a part of the old Confederation, but were allowed to drop out at this time, and were not included in the reorganization of Germany. This was true also of the tiny principality of Lichtenstein in the south.

[2] Von Sybel, *Begründung des Deutschen Reiches*, book xix. ch. ii.

[3] Also called Hesse-Cassel to distinguish it from Hesse-Darmstadt or grand-ducal Hesse, which, being the only Hesse remaining in existence as a separate State, is hereinafter called simply Hesse.

[4] The constitution of the Confederation was first agreed upon by the governments of the several States, then accepted with slight modifications by a National Assembly elected by universal suffrage for the purpose, and finally ratified by the legislatures of the States.

Diet, and composed in the same way of the plenipo-
tentiaries of the different States, but was endowed
with peculiar and extensive powers. Austria was excluded from all participation in German politics; while
the four States south of the Main — Bavaria, Wurtemberg, Baden, and Hesse[1] — became independent, and
were expressly left at liberty to form a separate union
among themselves. As a matter of fact, they made
offensive and defensive alliances with the Confederation, and formed with it a Zollverein or customs
union, whose organs were the two chambers of the
Confederation reinforced by representatives from the
southern States. Every one felt that the union of
Germany was incomplete so long as these States were
not a part of it; but Bavaria and Wurtemberg were
reluctant to surrender their independence; and the
enthusiasm aroused by the war with France in 1870
was required to raise the sentiment for German
nationality to such a pitch as to sweep them into line.
Even then they demanded and obtained special privileges as the price of their adhesion; but at last all
the difficulties were arranged, and in the autumn of
1870 treaties were made with the four southern States
whereby they joined the union. The name of the
Confederation was changed at the same time to that
of " German Empire," the president being The German
given the title of Emperor; and in the course Empire.
of the following winter the changes and additions

[1] This is Hesse-Darmstadt. It lay on both sides of the Main, but
the part on the north of that river was already included in the North
German Confederation.

entailed by these treaties were embodied in a new draft of the constitution.[1]

The constitution has nothing about it that is abstract

Practical character of the constitution. or ideal. It was drawn up by a man of affairs who knew precisely what he wanted, and understood very well the limitations imposed upon him, and the concessions he was obliged to make to the existing order of things. His prime object was to create a powerful military state, and hence, as has been pointed out, the articles on most subjects are comparatively meagre, but those on the army, the navy, and the revenue are drawn up with a minuteness befitting the by-laws of a commercial company.[2]

Before proceeding to a description of the organs of

---

[1] Cf. Laband, *Deutsches Staatsrecht*, 2d ed. ch. i.   In 1873 three amendments were made in this instrument. The first (that of Feb. 25) abolished the provision limiting the right to vote in the Reichstag, on those matters which by the constitution are not common to the whole Empire, to the representatives of the States affected. The second (that of March 3) put the lighthouses, buoys, etc., along the coast under the control of the federal government ; and the third (that of Dec. 20) extended the legislative power of the Empire over the whole field of civil and criminal law. It had previously covered contracts, commercial law, and criminal law. Except for a change in the term of the Reichstag in 1888 from three to five years, the constitution has remained unaltered since that time, but substantial changes in the fundamental law of the Empire have been made without a formal modification of the text. (See Laband, vol. i. pp. 48–49, 51.) Some of the German jurists maintain that such a practice is wrong (von Rönne, *Staatsrecht des Deutschen Reiches*, 2d ed. pp. 31–34; Meyer, *Lehrbuch des Deutschen Staatsrechts*, p. 416); others that it is quite proper, provided the majority required in the Bundesrath for a formal amendment of the constitution is in fact obtained. (Laband, vol. i. pp. 545–49; Arndt, *Verfassung des Deutschen Reiches*, pp. 290–91.) For the method of amending the constitution, see pages 246, 250–51, *infra*.

[2] Lebon, *Etudes sur l'Allemagne Politique*, Introd., p. iii.

the state, it will be worth while to examine the nature of the Confederation.   We are in the habit of speaking of the German Empire as a federal government, and rightly ; but we must bear in mind that it departs essentially from the type which we commonly associate with that term, and which is embodied in our own constitution.   We conceive of a federal system as one in which there is a division of powers between the central government and the States, according to subjects, so that in those matters which fall within the sphere of federal control the central government not only makes the laws, but executes them by means of its own officials.   Thus Congress enacts a tariff; the United States custom house collects the duties; and the federal courts decide the questions that arise under the law.   But all this is very different in Germany.   There the legislative power of the central government is far more extensive than in this country, for it includes almost everything that is placed under the control of Congress and many other matters besides.   In addition to such subjects as customs duties and taxes, the army and navy, the consular service, and the protection of foreign commerce, which are obviously essential, the list comprises many matters of domestic legislation.   It covers not only the posts and telegraphs,[1] transportation on streams running through more than one State, and extraditions between the States, but also in general terms railroads,[2] roads and canals, citizenship, travel,

Nature of the Confederation.

Large legislative and small executive powers.

---

[1] Except in Bavaria and Wurtemberg.
[2] Except in Bavaria.

change of residence, and the carrying on of trades, also the regulation of weights and measures, of coinage and paper money, and of banking, patents, copyrights, and of medical and veterinary police. Moreover, it includes the regulation of the press and associations, and finally the whole domain of ordinary civil and criminal law and of judicial proceedings. All these things are declared subject to imperial legislation and supervision.[1]

The administrative power of the Empire, on the other hand, is very small, the federal laws being carried out in the main by the officers of the States as under the Confederation of 1815. Except, indeed, for foreign affairs, the navy, and to some extent the army and the postal and telegraphic service, the executive functions of the Empire are limited for the most part to the laying down of general regulations, and a supervision of their execution by the several States.[2] Thus the federal government can enact a tariff, make regulations which shall govern the custom-house officers, and appoint inspectors to see that they are carried out; but the duties are actually collected by state officials.[3] One

---

[1] Art. 4 of the constitution and the amendment of Dec. 20, 1873.

[2] See Laband, § 66. In the case of the army (Const. Arts. 63–66) and the posts and telegraphs (Art. 50), the highest officers are appointed by the Emperor, who gives them their orders, while the subordinates are appointed by the States.

[3] As a rule the whole net revenue flows into the imperial treasury, but by the tariff act of 1879 the net revenue from customs duties above one hundred and thirty million marks is divided among the States in proportion to their population. In case the receipts of the Empire are not equal to its expenses, the deficiency is covered by means of contributions called *Matricularbeiträge* assessed on the different States in proportion to their

naturally asks what happens if a State refuses or fails
to carry out a federal law.   The matter is reported to
the Bundesrath, which decides any controversy about
the interpretation of the law.[1]   But suppose the State
persists in its refusal to administer the law, what can
the federal government do?   It cannot give effect to
the law itself, nor has it any officials for the purpose.
Its only resource is federal execution, — that is, an
armed attack on the delinquent State, — which can be
ordered by the Bundesrath, and is carried out by the
Emperor.[2]   This last resort has never been used, nor is
it likely to be, because the Emperor is also the King of
Prussia, and Prussia alone is not only larger than any
other State, but larger than all the rest put together.
Execution against Prussia is therefore doubly out of
the question; and any other State would be so easily
overpowered that it is certain to submit, rather than
provoke an appeal to force.

Another conception that we associate with federal
government is an equality of rights among the mem-

population. (Const. Art. 70, and see Laband, § 126.) This was originally
intended to be a subsidiary and exceptional source of revenue, but owing
to the quarrel between Bismarck and the Reichstag on the subject of
federal taxation, the Matricularbeiträge became large and permanent.
(Cf. Lebon, *Allemagne*, p. 106 *et seq.*) Under the present system the
excess of customs duties is paid to the States, and returned by them as
contributions, — a practice established in order to preserve the control of
the Reichstag over the imperial revenues, for the assessments upon the
States require a vote of that body, whereas the customs duties once voted
can be collected without further authorization, and the tariff cannot be
repealed without the consent of the Bundesrath, which for this purpose
is entirely subject to the will of the Emperor.   See page 247, *infra*.

[1] Const. Art. 7, § 3.
[2] Const. Art. 19, and see Laband, vol. i. pp. 105–6.

bers. But in the German Empire all is inequality. It

Inequality of rights among the members. would, indeed, have been impossible to make a federation on really equal terms between a number of States, one of which contained three fifths of the total population, while the other twenty-four contained altogether only two fifths. The compact could not fail to resemble that between the lion and the fox, or rather a compact between a lion,

Privileges of Prussia. half a dozen foxes, and a score of mice. The larger States are accorded all sorts of privileges, and so much of the lion's share of these falls to Prussia that it is hardly too much to say that she rules Germany with the advice and assistance of the other States. In the first place she has a perpetual right to have her King the Emperor of Germany.[1] Secondly,

Under the constitution. amendments to the constitution — although requiring only an ordinary majority vote in the Reichstag — are defeated in the Bundesrath if fourteen negative votes are thrown against them, and as Prussia has seventeen votes in that body, she has an absolute veto on all changes of the constitution.[2] Besides this, it is expressly provided that in the case of all bills relating to the army, the navy, the customs

[1] Const. Art. 11.

[2] Const. Art. 78. In the North German Confederation a two thirds vote in the Bundesrath was necessary for a change in the constitution, but when the South German States were admitted, Prussia had no longer a third of the delegates, and in order to preserve her veto the proportion required was increased to three quarters. Finally at the instance of Bavaria, which wanted to enlarge the power of the States of the second size, it was agreed that fourteen negative votes should be enough to defeat an amendment to the constitution. Arndt, p. 290; Robinson, *The German Bundesrath*, p. 40.

duties, or the excises, and in the case of all proposals to revise the administrative regulations for collecting the revenue, the vote of Prussia in the Bundesrath is decisive if cast in favor of maintaining the existing institutions.[1] In other words, Prussia has a veto on all measures for making changes in the army, the navy, or the taxes. She has also the casting vote in case of a tie in the Bundesrath,[2] and the chairmanship of all the standing committees of that body.[3]

These are Prussia's constitutional privileges; but she has others obtained by private agreement with her smaller partners; for the several States are at liberty to make conventions or treaties with each other in regard to the affairs that remain subject to their control.[4] When the North German Confederation was formed, universal military service and a uniform organization like that of Prussia were introduced into all the States, but the army was not made exclusively a national or left entirely a state institution.[5] The constitution provides that the military laws shall be made by the Empire,[6] and

And by special conventions with the other States.

The army.

---

[1] Const. Arts. 5, 35, and 37.   [2] Const. Art. 7.

[3] Const. Art. 8; Laband, vol i. p. 264. Except the committee on foreign affairs, where, as will be explained hereafter, it would be of no use to her.

[4] Laband, § 63. To some extent the States are at liberty to make separate conventions with foreign powers, and they have a right to send their own representatives to foreign courts. Laband, § 71.

[5] Const. Arts. 57–68. The last eight of these articles do not apply to Bavaria, and only partially to Wurtemberg. See page 250, *infra*. The expense of maintaining the army is borne by the Empire. Unlike the army, the navy is a purely national institution. Art. 53.

[6] The double position of the Prussian monarch comes out curiously here, for the constitution provides : first, that the military laws and regu-

declares that the forces of the country shall be a single
army under the command of the Emperor, whose orders
they are bound to obey. It gives him a right to inspect
and dispose of the troops, and to appoint all officers
whose command includes the entire contingent of a
State. It provides also that the selection of the gen-
erals shall be subject to his approval, but it leaves to
the States the appointment of all inferior officers, and
the management of their troops in other respects. Now
these reserved rights were of little value, and all but
three of the States transferred them to Prussia, chiefly
in consideration of an agreement on the part of the
Emperor not to remove the troops from their own territory except in case of actual necessity. Thus the
contingents of these States are recruited, drilled, and
commanded by Prussia, and form, in short, an integral
part of her army.[1]

A number of conventions of a similiar character, affecting other public matters, such as the postal service and the jurisdiction of the courts,
have been concluded between the States; but

Convention
with Wal-
deck.

lations of Prussia shall be in force throughout the Empire ; second, that
thereafter a comprehensive imperial military law shall be enacted;
and third that any future general orders of the Prussian army shall
be communicated by the military committee of the Bundesrath to the
commanders of the other contingents for appropriate imitation.

[1] Some of the States transferred all their rights (Baden with a provision that her troops should form a separate corps) ; others retained
certain rights, mainly of an honorary nature, but agreed that their
troops should be united with the Prussian army, and that Prussia should
appoint the officers. Only Bavaria, Saxony, and Wurtemberg still exercise the military functions reserved to them by the constitution. Cf.
Laband, § 94, iii. ; Schulze, *Lehrbuch des Deutschen Staatsrechts*, § 335;
Meyer, *Lehrbuch*, § 197.

the most comprehensive compact of all was made by Waldeck. The ruler of this little principality was crippled with debts, and unable to raise the money required for the reorganization of his army. So he sold his governmental rights as a whole to the King of Prussia, retired from business, and went to Italy to live upon his income, while the Prussian government, having bought the good-will of his trade, proceeded to carry it on as his successor. There is something decidedly comical in treating the right to govern a community as a marketable commodity, to be bought and sold for cash; but to Bismarck the matter presented itself as a perfectly natural business transaction, and in fact the contract bears a strong resemblance to the lease of a small American railroad to a larger one.

Such are the special privileges of Prussia. Those reserved to the other States are far less extensive. By the constitution Hamburg and Bremen had a right to remain free ports, outside of the operation of the tariff laws; [1] but both of them have now surrendered this privilege. [2] The other special rights are mostly enjoyed by the southern States, and were given to them as an inducement to join the Confederation. Thus Bavaria,

Privileges of the other States.

Hamburg and Bremen.

---

[1] Const. Art. 34.

[2] The treaty for this purpose was made with Hamburg in 1881, and went into effect Oct. 1, 1888. That with Bremen was made in 1885. For an account of these treaties and the way they were brought about, see Blum, *Das Deutsche Reich zur Zeit Bismarck's*, p. 360 *et seq.*; Laband, vol. ii. pp. 901–4.

Wurtemberg, and Baden are exempt from imperial excises on brandy and beer, and have a right
to lay excises of their own on these articles.[1]

Bavaria,
Wurtem-
berg, and
Baden.

Bavaria and Wurtemberg have their own
postal and telegraph services, which are subject only to
general imperial laws.[2] Except for the principle of
universal military service, and the agreement to conform to the general organization of the imperial army,
Bavaria has in time of peace the entire charge of her
own troops, the Emperor having only a right to inspect
them; while Wurtemberg, although not so much favored as this, has greater military privileges than the
remaining States.[3] Bavaria is further exempt from
imperial legislation in regard to railroads,[4] and to residence and settlement;[5] and finally, by the constitution or by military convention, Bavaria, Saxony, and
Wurtemberg have a right to seats on the committees
of the Bundesrath on foreign affairs and on the army
and fortresses.[6] In order to guarantee more effectually
these privileges, it is provided that they shall not be

---

[1] Const. Art. 35. But in 1887 they gave up their privileges in regard
to brandy. See Blum, p. 532 ; Laband, vol. ii. pp. 920, 923–24.

[2] Const. Art. 52.

[3] Treaties of Nov. 23, 1870, with Bavaria ; and Nov. 25, 1870, with
Wurtemberg ; incorporated in the constitution by a reference in the Ap-
pendix to Part XI.

[4] Except in the case of lines that have a strategic importance. Const.
Art. 46.

[5] Const. Art. 4, § 1.

[6] Const. Art. 8 ; Laband, vol. i. p. 113. By the treaty of Nov. 23,
1870 (Schlussprotokoll, Art. ix.), Bavaria has a right to preside over the
Bundesrath in the absence of Prussia, but as this never happens, the privilege is merely honorary.

changed without the consent of the State entitled to them.[1]

From this description of the privileges of the different States it is evident that the German Empire is very far from being a federal union of the kind with which we are familiar. It is rather a continuation of the old Germanic Confederation, with the centre of gravity shifted from the States to the central government, and the preponderating power placed in the hands of Prussia, — the other large States retaining privileges roughly in proportion to their size.[2]

The empire a continuation of the old Confederation in a modified form.

Its organs.

---

[1] Const. Art. 78. Meyer (*Lehrbuch,* p. 421) and Zorn (*Staatsrecht des Deutschen Reiches,* pp. 88–93) think this provision applies only to the limitations on the competence of the Empire, and not to the privileges given to the several States in the organization of the government, such as the presidential rights of Prussia, the allotment of the votes in the Bundesrath, the seats on committees, etc. Their opinion, however, is not generally accepted. Laband, vol. i. pp. 110–14 ; Schulze, § 249 ; v. Rönne, vol. ii. pp. 43–48. It is universally agreed that an affirmative vote in the Bundesrath by the delegate of the State is a sufficient consent by that State to a law affecting its privileges so far as the Empire is concerned ; but there is a difference of opinion on the question how far the ruler of the State is bound, or can be bound, by state law to consult his parliament. Laband, vol. i. pp. 114–17 ; Schulze, bk. ii. p. 19 ; v. Rönne, vol. ii. pp. 36–43 ; Meyer, p. 422 ; Zorn, pp. 94–98.

[2] In saying this I am speaking only of the political structure of the government, and do not mean to touch the philosophical question whether the sovereignty has or has not been transferred from the States to the Empire. This point has been the subject of elaborate argument, and in fact the same juristic questions about the origin and nature of the federal government have been discussed in Germany as in the United States. (For a reference to these discussions see Laband, vol. i. pp. 30–33, 52 *et seq.,* and see especially Jellinek, *Die Lehre von den Staatenverbindungen.*) Some of the German publicists maintain that the sovereignty resides in the Bundesrath, a view which, as Burgess points out in his

Its chief organ of government is still the old Diet, re-
named the Bundesrath or Federal Council, to which
have been added on one side an Emperor, who is commander-in-chief of the forces, and represents the Empire in its relation with foreign powers; and, on the
other, an elected chamber, called the Reichstag, created
for the sake of stimulating national sentiment and
enlisting popular support as against the local and dy-
nastic influences which have free play in the Bundesrath.   Let us consider each of these organs in detail.

The Reichstag is elected for five years by direct
universal suffrage and secret ballot.[1]   The
voters must be twenty-five years old, and not
in active military service, paupers, or otherwise disqualified.[2]   The members are chosen in single electoral districts fixed by imperial law.[3]   These
had originally a hundred thousand inhabitants apiece,[4]
but they have not been revised for more than a score
of years, and with the growth of the large cities have
gradually become very unequal.   In the case of Berlin
the disproportion is enormous, for the city has now
nearly two million and a half inhabitants, but is still rep-

*The
Reichstag.*

*Its compo-
sition.*

Political Science (vol. ii. pp. 90–93) is somewhat artificial. For those who
think as I do, that sovereignty is not in its nature indivisible, the question
loses much of its importance. (Cf. *Essays on Government*, chapter on the
Limits of Sovereignty.)

[1] Cf. Laband, § 34 ; Const. Arts. 20, 24. Until 1888 the period was
three years.

[2] Wahlgesetz, May 31, 1869, §§ 1–3. Every voter who has been a
citizen of any State for a year is eligible in any district in the Empire
without regard to residence. Soldiers in active service, though not allowed to vote, are eligible. (*Id.*, § 4.)

[3] Wahlgesetz, § 6.   [4] Except in the smallest States.

resented by only six members. The government, however, is not anxious for a redistribution of seats, because Berlin elects Radicals and Socialists, who form
a troublesome opposition, — a tendency which is also
true of other large centres. As in the United States,
no district can be composed of parts of different States,
so that every State, however small, elects at least one
representative. The three hundred and ninety-seven
seats are in fact distributed as follows : Prussia has
two hundred and thirty-five, or about three fifths of
the whole number, Bavaria forty-eight, Saxony twenty-
three, Wurtemberg seventeen, Alsace-Lorraine fifteen,
Baden fourteen, Hesse nine, Mecklenburg-Schwerin six,
Saxe-Weimar three, Oldenburg three, Brunswick three,
Hamburg three, Saxe-Meiningen two, Saxe-Coburg-
Gotha two, Anhalt two, and all the rest one each.[1] As
regards the method of election the system of *ballotage*
prevails; that is, an absolute majority is required for
election on the first ballot, and if no one obtains this,
a second ballot takes place which is confined to the
two candidates who have received the largest number
of votes.[2]

Universal suffrage was looked upon as an experiment of a somewhat hazardous character, and Payment of
Bismarck insisted on the non-payment of the members.
members of the Reichstag as a safeguard.[3] This was

---

[1] Wahlgesetz, § 5 ; Const. Art. 20 ; Act of June 25, 1873 (Alsace-
Lorraine), § 3.

[2] Wahlgesetz, § 12. Lebon (p. 82) thinks this last provision, by cut-
ting out all the candidates but the two highest on the list, favors the
government and hampers the free expression of opinion.

[3] Const. Art. 32.

a bone of contention with the Liberals for many years, — the Reichstag having repeatedly passed bills for the payment of members, which the Bundesrath until 1906 rejected.[1] The absence of remuneration has not been without effect, for it has deterred university professors and other men of small means, usually of liberal views, from accepting an office which entails the expense of a long residence in Berlin, but it has not fulfilled the predictions that were made either by its foes or its friends, for it has not caused a dearth of candidates, or discouraged the presence of men who make politics their occupation. The provision has, however, a meaning one would hardly suspect. In 1885, when the Socialist representatives were paid a salary by their own party, Bismarck, claiming that such a proceeding was illegal, caused the treasury to sue them for the sums of money they had received in this way, and, strange to say, the Imperial Court of Appeal sustained the suits. The object of withholding pay from the members is, of course, to prevent the power of the poorer classes from becoming too great; but a much more effectual means to the same end is the habit of holding elections on working days, instead of holding them on Sundays, as is done in France and most of the other Catholic countries.

[1] In 1906 a measure providing for the payment of members was enacted. Since that date a nominal allowance of 3000 marks (about $750) per year has been paid, with a reduction of 25 marks for each day's absence. The annual allowance is hardly large enough to be termed a salary.

The Reichstag has the ordinary privileges of a legislative assembly, electing its own president, The com-
making its own rules, and deciding upon the mittee sys-
validity of elections.[1] Its internal organiza- tem.
tion conforms to the pattern generally followed in continental chambers. At the beginning of each session
the members are divided by lot into seven *Abthei-
lungen* or sections, which correspond to the Bureaux
of the French Chambers, but differ from these in the
important respect that they last during the whole
session, instead of being renewed at short intervals.
The duties of the sections consist in making a preliminary examination of the validity of elections to the
Reichstag, and in the choice of committees, each section
electing one or more committee-men, according to the
importance of the committee.[2] As in France and Italy,
however, the choice by the sections is really cut and dried
beforehand. It is in fact controlled by the Senioren-
Convent, a body composed of the leaders of the different parties, who determine in advance the number
of seats on the committee to which each party shall
be entitled.[3] Bills are not always referred to a committee; but it is noteworthy that the more advanced
Liberals have constantly urged such a reference in
the case of government bills, because the authoritative
influence of the ministers is thereby diminished, and
greater opportunity is given for criticism and amend-

[1] Const. Art. 27.

[2] Laband, vol. ii. pp. 327–29. Unlike the French Bureaux, their choice
is not confined to members of their own section. Lebon, p. 88.

[3] Lebon, *Ib.*; Dupriez, vol. i. p. 526 ; Laband, vol. i. p. 328.

ment; while the more moderate parties, following the lead of the government, have often preferred an immediate discussion of important measures by the full house, without the intervention of any committee at all.

The powers of the Reichstag appear very great on paper. All laws require its consent, and so

The powers of the Reichstag. do the budget, all loans, and all treaties which involve matters falling within the domain of legislation. It has a right to initiate legislation, to ask the government for reports, and to express its opinion on the management of affairs.[1] In reality, however, its powers are not so great as they seem. The constitution provides, for example, that the budget shall be annual,[2] but the principal revenue laws are permanent, and cannot be changed without the consent of the Bundesrath,[3] while the most important appropriation, that for the army, is virtually determined by the law fixing the number of the troops, and this has hitherto been voted for a number of years at a time.[4] The chief function of the Reichstag is, in fact, the consideration of bills prepared by the Chancellor and the Bundesrath. These it criticises and amends pretty freely; but its activity is rather negative than positive, and although important measures have occasionally

[1] Const. Arts. 5, 11, 23, 69, 73 ; Laband, § 33.

[2] In 1867 Bismarck wanted triennial sessions, and in 1888, when the term of the Reichstag was changed to five years, he wanted the sessions held only every other year.

[3] It is to be remembered, moreover, that the bulk of the civil administration is in the hands of the States, which provide the means of carrying it on.

[4] In 1871, for three years ; in 1874, 1880, and 1887 for seven years; and since 1893 for five years.

been passed at its instigation,[1] it cannot be said to direct the policy of the state either in legislation or administration.[2]

The influence of the Reichstag is also diminished by the fact that it can be dissolved at any time by the Bundesrath with the consent of the Emperor.[3] In most constitutional governments at the present day the power of dissolution is the complement of the responsibility of the ministers, and is used, at least in theory, to ascertain whether the cabinet possesses the confidence of the nation. But in Germany it exists without any such responsibility, and hence is simply a means of breaking down resistance in the Reichstag. It has, indeed, been used for this purpose on three memorable occasions: first, in 1878, when the Reichstag refused to pass a bill for the repression of agitation by the Socialists; afterwards in 1887, when it refused to pass the bill fixing the size of the army for seven years; and again in 1893, when it refused to sanction changes proposed in the military system. In each case the new Reichstag supported the plans of the government, and thus a serious conflict with the Chancellor was avoided, and the

The right of dissolution.

[1] A striking example of this was the amendment to Art. 4 of the constitution extending the competence of the Empire to ordinary civil and criminal law.

[2] Cf. Lebon, pp. 113–16. The debate in the budget is used as an occasion for criticism of the government, and for the expression of opinion, but in the budget itself few changes are made. The reductions have little importance, while the rejection of an appropriation asked for is extremely rare, and an increase is almost unknown. Dupriez, vol. i. pp. 543–44.

[3] Const. Art. 24.

question of the ultimate authority of the different organs of the state was postponed.

The rules of the Reichstag provide for interpellations, but the question to whom these shall be addressed involves one of the paradoxes, or contradictions between theory and practice, which are common in the government of the Empire. There is no imperial cabinet, and the Chancellor, who is the only minister, has no right, as such, to sit in the Reichstag. In theory he comes there only as one of the delegates to the Bundesrath,—all whose members have the privilege of being present in the Reichstag, where a special bench is reserved for them. They appear as the representatives of the united governments of Germany, and are entitled to speak whenever they choose; for the Bundesrath is not only a collection of delegates from the governments of the different States, but has also some of the attributes of an imperial cabinet. In form, therefore, interpellations are addressed to the Bundesrath, but in fact they are communicated to the Chancellor, who usually answers them himself, or allows one of his subordinates to do so. A debate may ensue if demanded by fifty members, but it is not followed by an order of the day expressing the opinion of the House,[1] and, indeed, interpellations have no such importance as in France and Italy, because the parliamentary system does not exist; that is, the

Interpellations.

---

[1] Lebon, p. 105; v. Rönne, p. 268. A resolution can, of course, be moved in accordance with the ordinary rules of procedure, and this was done on the occasion of the expulsion of the Poles in Jan., 1886. Blum, pp. 498–501. Dupriez (vol. i. p. 545) comments on the Polish incident.

Chancellor does not resign on an adverse vote of the Reichstag, nor does he feel obliged to conform to its wishes.

Let us now examine more closely the Bundesrath, — that extraordinary mixture of legislative chamber, executive council, court of appeal, and permanent assembly of diplomats. It is the most thoroughly native feature of the German Empire, and has, therefore, a peculiar vitality. The Bundesrath is composed of delegates appointed by the princes of the States and the senates of the Free Cities;[1] and it is to be observed that Alsace-Lorraine, which was taken from France in 1871, is not strictly a member of the union, but only *Reichsland* or imperial territory, and hence has no right to a representative in the Bundesrath, although as a part of the empire it elects members of the Reichstag. Its position is in some ways analogous to that of one of our Territories, while the other parts of the Empire correspond to our States. Curiously enough, Alsace-Lorraine has been allowed since 1879 to send to the Bundesrath delegates who, like the representatives of the Territories in Congress, can debate, but cannot vote.[2]

The seats in the Bundesrath are distributed among the States and Cities in such a way that each of them is entitled to the same number of votes as in the

The Bundesrath.

Its composition.

[1] Const. Arts. 6–10.

[2] Laband, vol. i. pp. 219–20. In the law of 1879, as originally drawn up by Bismarck, Alsace-Lorraine was entitled to ordinary delegates to the Bundesrath ; but that body, in order not to increase the seats virtually controlled by the King of Prussia, insisted that they should have no vote. Blum, pp. 635–36. The number of these delegates is four.

diet of the old Germanic Confederation when that body proceeded *in plenum ;* except that Bavaria, as part of the inducement to join the Empire, was given six delegates instead of four,[1] and Prussia obtained those of the States she absorbed in 1866.[2]

There are in all fifty-eight members, of which Prussia has seventeen, Bavaria six, Saxony and Wurtemberg four each, Baden and Hesse three each, Brunswick and Mecklenburg-Schwerin two each, and the remaining fourteen States and three Free Cities one each. But Prussia has really three votes more, because the contract for the government of Waldeck already mentioned gave her the vote of that State, and in 1884–85 she caused the Duke of Cumberland to be excluded from the succession in Brunswick, got a Prussian prince appointed perpetual regent, and thus obtained the virtual control of these two votes also;[3] so that she has in reality twenty votes out of the fifty-eight. This, of course, is much less than her proportion of the population ;[4] but twenty votes in the same hand count

[1] She had six votes in the Bundesrath of the Zollverein from 1866 to 1871.

[2] Laband, vol. i. p. 220. The votes acquired by Prussia in this way were those of Hanover, 4 ; Hesse Cassel, 3 ; Holstein-Lauenburg, 3 ; Nassau, 2 ; and Frankfort, 1.

[3] The Duke was excluded because as son and heir of the late King of Hanover he insisted on his right to that kingdom, and refused to acknowledge its incorporation in Prussia. His son, who married the Emperor's daughter, has recently been restored to the dukedom.

[4] The population of Germany on Dec. 1, 1890, was about forty-nine millions, of which Prussia had thirty millions, Bavaria five millions and a half, Saxony three millions and a half, Wurtemberg two millions, Alsace-Lorraine and Baden a million and a half apiece, Hesse one million, and the other nineteen States together four millions.

far more than the same number held by different
States, and she has only to win ten additional votes, —
those of Bavaria and Wurtemberg, for example, or
those of some of the smaller States, — in order to
have an absolute majority. In fact, she has usually
had her way, although on several notable occasions the
other States have combined and defeated her. This
happened in 1877, when the seat of the Imperial
Court of Appeal was fixed at Leipsic instead of Berlin
as she desired;[1] and in 1876 on the more important
question of the imperial railroad law. At that time
Bismarck refrained altogether from introducing into
the Bundesrath a bill for the purchase of railroads by
the Empire, knowing that it would be defeated by the
opposition of the middle-sized States, although the
project was one on which he had set his heart.[2]
Again, in 1879, another railroad bill was killed in the
Bundesrath by the opposition of Bavaria, Saxony, and
Wurtomberg,[3] and in the same year a conference of
the finance ministers of the States refused to consent
to the tobacco monopoly.[4]

The members of the Bundesrath are diplomats rather
than senators.[5] They enjoy at Berlin the privileges of
foreign ambassadors, and are appointed and removed

[1] Cf. Blum, pp. 146–47. The vote in favor of Leipsic was thirty to
twenty-eight; and it is noteworthy that if Prussia had then controlled
the votes of Brunswick the majority would have been the other way.

[2] Cf. Blum, pp. 165–68.

[3] Blum, p. 345.

[4] Blum, p. 312. On this point, however, they yielded some years later.

[5] The constitution (Art. 10) provides that the Emperor shall vouchsafe
to them the protection accorded to ambassadors, while the members of
the Reichstag have the ordinary privileges of members of a parliament.

at will by the States they represent, — which also pay
them or not as they please. The votes they

Character of the Bundesrath and the position of its members. cast are the votes of the States, not those
of its representatives, and it is therefore pro-
vided that all the delegates of a State must
vote alike. In fact, all the votes belonging to a State
are counted without reference to the number of delegates actually voting;[1] and thus the seventeen votes
of Prussia, for example, can be cast in her name by a
single representative, just as at the meeting of a private corporation a properly authorized agent can vote
on all the shares of stock belonging to his principal.
The delegates, moreover, vote according to the instructions of their home government, and the constitution expressly declares that votes not instructed shall
not be counted.[2] This last provision has given rise to
some comment. It does not mean that a delegate must
produce his instructions before he is allowed to vote.
On the contrary, the Bundesrath appears to take no
cognizance of instructions, which may, indeed, be of
any kind, including an authority to vote as the delegate
thinks best; and it is even asserted that a vote is valid
whether it is in accord with the instructions or not.[3]
The provision in the constitution is probably a mere
survival; but it has been suggested that its object is,
on the one hand, to allow a delegate to excuse himself
from voting on the plea that he has not been instructed,
and on the other to make it clear that a vote can be
taken, although the delegates have not all received

[1] Laband, vol. i. p. 223. [2] Const. Art. 7.
[3] Laband, vol. i. p. 229.

their instructions, thus taking away an excuse for delay that might otherwise be urged.[1]

A delegate is usually an officer of the State he represents, often one of its ministers, or even the head of its cabinet, and in any case the ministers of a State are responsible according to its own laws for their instructions to the delegates.[2] In fact, the ministers are frequently questioned in the local Landtag or legislature, about the instructions they have given, or propose to give; and resolutions are sometimes passed in regard to them.[3] If, indeed, the strict parliamentary system existed in any of the German States, the cabinet would no doubt be held responsible to the Landtag for these instructions as for every other act of the government.

Although the delegates are frequently officers of the State they represent, they are not necessarily even citizens of it; and it is not uncommon for several of the smaller States, from motives of economy, to empower the same man to act as delegate for them all jointly. This habit grew to such an extent that in April, 1880, when a stamp act proposed by the Chancellor was seriously amended by a vote of thirty to twenty-eight, thirteen of the smaller States were not represented by any delegates of their own, their votes being cast by two delegates from other States. Bismarck tendered his resignation in disgust, and this

[1] Cf. Robinson, "The German Bundesrath," *Pub. Univ., Pa. Pub. Law Series*, vol. iii. no. 1, pp. 34–35.

[2] Laband, vol. i. pp. 225–27.

[3] Interpellations, for example, were presented and answered in several States in regard to the proposal for the purchase of railroads by the Empire, to which allusion has already been made (Blum, p. 167).

caused the Bundesrath to reconsider its action and vote the tax. But the Chancellor was not satisfied. He complained that the practice of substitution deprived the Bundesrath of the presence of members who were open to argument, and he insisted on the adoption of a rule dividing the session into two periods, in one of which the important matters should be considered, and delegates from all the States should be present, while the other should be devoted to current affairs, when the States might appoint substitutes if they pleased. This rule was adopted, and for the convenience of the delegates the former period is made as short as possible.[1]

The Bundesrath is in its nature unlike any other body in the world, and its peculiarities can be explained only by a reference to the Diet of the old Germanic Confederation. It is not an international conference, because it is part of a constitutional system, and has power to enact laws. On the other hand, it is not a deliberative assembly, because the delegates vote according to instructions from home. It is unlike any other legislative chamber, inasmuch as the members do not enjoy a fixed tenure of office, and are not free to vote according to their personal convictions. Its essential characteristics are that it represents the governments of the States and not their people, and that each State is entitled to a certain number of votes which it may authorize one or more persons to cast in its name, these persons being its agents, whom it may appoint, recall, or instruct at any time. The true conception of

[1] Blum, pp. 348–49; Laband, vol. i. pp. 256–57.

the Bundesrath, therefore, is that of an assembly of the sovereigns of the States, who are not, indeed, actually present, but appear in the persons of their representatives.

The internal organization of the Bundesrath is in accord with its federal character and the privileged position of the larger States. We have already seen that the seventeen votes of Prussia are more than enough to defeat any constitutional amendment, and that she is expressly given a veto on all proposals to change the laws relating to the army or the taxes. Besides this, the constitution declares that the Emperor, that is, the King of Prussia, shall appoint the Chancellor, who presides over the body and arranges its business, and through whose hands all communications from the Reichstag and all motions and petitions must pass,[1] and who is in fact always one of the Prussian delegates.[2] But the constitution goes into much smaller details in regulating privileges of the States, and prescribes even the composition of the committees; for the Germans have shown a remarkable astuteness in this matter, and nowhere else in the world can we find

The internal organization of the Bundesrath.

The committees.

---

[1] Const. Art. 15. Cf. Robinson, p. 37.

[2] Most of the German jurists argue that the Chancellor must always be a Prussian delegate, because Art. 15 of the constitution implies that he must be a member of the Bundesrath, and the Emperor has power to create such members only in his capacity as King of Prussia. Laband, vol. i. pp. 253–54; Meyer, *Lehrbuch*, § 124; Schulze, vol. ii. p. 91. Hensel (*Die Stellung des Reichskanzlers*, pp. 10–12) denies this and quotes Bismarck in his favor. The Chancellor is authorized to commit the duty of acting as chairman to a substitute, and in fact he rarely presides in person. See Dupriez, vol. i. p. 522, and Blum, p. 143.

the important influence of committees in a legislative body so thoroughly recognized. There are eight standing committees of the Bundesrath established by the constitution.[1] The members of one of these — that on the army and fortresses — are appointed by the Emperor; but it is provided by the constitution that Bavaria, and by military convention that Saxony and Wurtemberg, shall have places upon it. The members of the committee on maritime affairs are also appointed by the Emperor; while the committees on taxes and customs, on trade, on railroads, posts and telegraphs, on justice, and on accounts, are elected every year by the Bundesrath itself. On each of the last seven committees, five States at least must be represented, of which one must always be Prussia, whose member is always the chairman. But here again we have an illustration of the fact that the Bundesrath is an assembly of diplomats and not of senators, for the practice followed by the Emperor or the Bundesrath — whichever has the power of appointment — is to designate the States to be represented, and the delegation from each of those States chooses one of its own members to sit on the committee. The seat on a committee belongs, therefore, not to the representative selected, but to the State which he represents. There is one other committee provided for by the constitution, — that on foreign affairs. Its functions are peculiar; for it does not report like the other committees, but its members listen to the communications made to them by the Chancellor, and express the views of their

[1] Const. Art. 8.

respective governments thereon. It is thus in reality a means by which the ministers of the larger States may be consulted upon foreign affairs; and it consists of representatives of Bavaria, Saxony, Wurtemberg, and two other States designated every year by the Bundesrath. As its only function is to consult with the Chancellor, who is virtually the Prussian minister for foreign affairs, Prussia has no seat upon it, and in her absence Bavaria presides.[1]

Another illustration of the federal character of the Bundesrath is to be found in the provision that on matters not common to the whole Empire, — such, for example, as the excise on beer, from which Bavaria, Wurtemberg, and Baden enjoy an exemption, — only those States which are interested can vote.[2] There was at first a similar provision for the Reichstag, but it was felt to be inconsistent with the spirit of a national house of representatives, and was repealed.[3]

Only delegates of the States interested allowed to vote.

The powers of the Bundesrath are very extensive, and cover nearly the whole field of government. It is a part of the legislature, and every law requires its assent.[4] But, more

Powers of the Bundesrath.

[1] There are also three standing committees not provided for by the constitution : those on Alsace-Lorraine, on the constitution, and on rules. All the standing committees may sit when the Bundesrath is not in session. On the subject of the committees, see Laband, § 31.

[2] Const. Art. 7.

[3] Amend. Feb. 24, 1873.

[4] Including treaties that fall within the domain of legislation, Const. Art. 11. Each State has the right of initiative (Art. 7), which is, of course, most frequently used by Prussia.

than this, it has the first and last word on almost all the laws, for the Reichstag has not succeeded in making its right of initiative in legislation very effective, and by far the larger part of the statutes (as well as the budget) are prepared and first discussed by the Bundesrath. They are then sent to the Reichstag, and if passed by that body, are again submitted to the Bundesrath for approval before they are promulgated by the Emperor.[1] The Bundesrath may therefore be said to be not only a part of the legislature, but the main source of legislation.

Legislative.

It is also a part of the executive. As such, it has power to make regulations for the conduct of the administration, and to issue ordinances for the completion of the laws, so far as this power has not been specially lodged by statute in other hands.[2] In regard to finance its authority is even more extensive, for it has been given many of the functions of a chamber of accounts.[3] It enjoys a share of the power of appointment, for it nominates among other officials the judges of the Imperial Court, and elects the members of the Court of Accounts; while collectors of

Executive.

[1] Laband, vol. i. p. 542 ; Schulze, vol. ii. p. 118.

[2] Const. Art. 7. It exercises this power with great freedom. Robinson, pp. 50–53. There is some difference of opinion how far this power extends. Laband, vol. i. pp. 236–37 ; v. Rönne, vol. i. pp. 213–15 ; Arndt, pp. 115–19. Arndt has also published a treatise on this subject, *Das Verordnungsrecht des Deutschen Reiches.* It is also empowered to decide upon defects that appear in the execution of the laws. Const. Art. 7, § 3. The meaning of this clause has been much discussed. Laband, vol. i. pp. 238–42, 246 ; v. Rönne, vol. i. pp. 215–16 ; Arndt, *Verfassung des Deutschen Reiches,* p. 119 ; Robinson, pp. 56–59.

[3] Laband, vol. i. pp. 244–46.

taxes and consuls can be appointed only with the approbation of its committees.[1] Under this head of executive power must also be classed the provisions by which its consent is required for a declaration of war,[2] for a dissolution of the Reichstag,[3] and for federal execution against a refractory State.[4] The Bundesrath, moreover, acts in some ways like a ministry of state, for it designates one or more of its members to support in the Reichstag the measures it has approved; and in fact a practice has grown up of informing the Reichstag during the progress of a debate what amendments to a bill the Bundesrath is willing to accept.[5] But the federal nature of the Bundesrath comes into play again curiously here, for each of the members also represents in the Reichstag his particular government, and can express its views, although contrary to those of a majority of his colleagues.[6]

The Bundesrath has no little power of a judicial or semi-judicial nature. It decides disputes between the imperial and state governments   Judicial. about the interpretation of imperial statutes.[7] It is virtually a court of appeal in cases where there is a denial of justice by a state court.[8] It decides controversies between States, which are not of the nature

---

[1] Laband, vol. i. pp. 242–43.

[2] Except on the ground that an attack has been made on the territory of the Empire. Const. Art. 11.

[3] Const. Art. 24.

[4] Const. Art. 19.

[5] Laband, vol. i. p. 537, n. 5.

[6] Const. Art. 9.

[7] This is deduced from Const. Art. 7, § 3.   See page 268, note 2, *supra*.

[8] Art. 77.

of private law, if appealed to by one of the parties;[1] and, finally, when a constitutional question arises in a State which has no tribunal empowered to decide it, the Bundesrath must try to settle it by mediation if requested to do so by one of the parties, or if this fails, it must try to dispose of the matter by imperial legislation.[2]

The Bundesrath has not only far more extensive powers than the Reichstag, but it has also certain privileges that enhance its prestige and increase its authority. Thus the Reichstag cannot be summoned to meet without the Bundesrath, whereas the latter can sit alone, and must in fact be called together at any time on the request of one third of its members.[3] Unlike the Reichstag, moreover, the order of business in the Bundesrath is not broken off by the ending of the session, but is continuous, so that matters are taken up again at the point where they were left, and thus its work is made far more effective.[4] The most important privilege it enjoys, however, is that of excluding the public from its meetings.[5] This has given it the

Special privileges of the Bundesrath.

Privacy of meetings.

---

[1] Const. Art. 76. If unfitted to decide the question, it can substitute for itself some other body, and this it did in 1877 in the case of the controversy between Prussia and Saxony in regard to the Berlin-Dresden railroad, selecting the Court of Appeal of Lübeck. Laband, vol. i. p. 249, note 2.

[2] Const. Art. 76, § 2.

[3] Const. Arts. 13–14.

[4] Laband, vol. i. p. 253.

[5] The constitution does not provide whether the sessions shall be public or not, and in fact they have always been secret (v. Rönne, vol. i. pp. 210–11). A brief report of the matters dealt with and the conclusions

advantage of concealing to some extent its internal differences, and has enabled it to acquire a reputation for greater unanimity, and consequently to exert more influence than it would otherwise possess. Privacy, indeed, would seem to be almost as essential to the Bundesrath, as to the cabinet in a parliamentary government, or to an Anglo-Saxon jury. It is easy to perceive that the twelve jurors would seldom agree, if the public were allowed to witness the mysterious process of reaching a verdict; and it is equally clear that harmony in the Bundesrath would be very seriously imperiled, if its galleries were filled with spectators. One can imagine how the newspapers would gloat over the last altercation between the Chancellor and the representative of Bavaria or Saxony, and how hard it would be for the contending parties to make the concessions necessary to effect an agreement after their differences had been discussed in public. The work of the Bundesrath must be an unending series of compromises, and a compromise is a thing with which the world at large has little sympathy. If, therefore, the meetings of the Bundesrath were open, it would be a hotbed of dissensions between the governments of the different States, instead of a bond of union and a means of mutual understanding.

In regard to the power and influence actually wielded by the Bundesrath, the most contradictory state-

reached is given to the press after each session, but the Bundesrath can vote to withhold from the public all information about any matter, and the rules provide that the oral proceedings both in the Bundesrath and its committees shall be kept secret in all cases. Laband, vol. i. p. 259.

ments are made. It is said on the one hand to be the
most important body in the Empire,[1] and on
the other that it is a mere nullity which
moves almost entirely at the dictation of
Prussia.[2] Both these statements are largely true, for
considered as an independent council with a will of
its own the Bundesrath is a nullity, because it derives
its impulse exclusively from outside forces; but, considered as an instrument by means of which the
governments of the larger States, and especially of
Prussia, rule the nation, it is probably the most important, although the least conspicuous, organ in the
Empire. The extent of Prussia's authority in the
Bundesrath cannot be accurately determined, owing to
the secrecy of the proceedings. That her will, or rather
the will of the Chancellor acting in her name, is the
chief moving and directing force, is evident; but that
he is not influenced by the opinions of the other States,
that he does not modify his plans in consequence of
their objections, or make compromises with them on
contested points, it seems hazardous to assert. The
members are usually wise enough not to talk about
their differences in public, and hence these are only
partly known to the world. At one time the minister
of Wurtemberg complained openly in the Reichstag
that bills were presented to the Bundesrath drawn up
in a complete form by Prussian officials, and filled
exclusively with a Prussian spirit;[3] but we know that

Actual in-fluence of the Bundes-rath.

[1] Robinson, p. 43.
[2] Lebon, pp. 145–51 ; Dupriez, vol. i. pp. 478, 517–23.
[3] See Blum, p. 140.

this has not always been the case, and that important measures have frequently been considered and discussed by the ministers of all the larger States before they were introduced at all.[1] We know also that in more than one instance Bismarck found it impossible to persuade the Bundesrath to adopt his views,[2] and that on another occasion he thought a threat of resignation necessary to compel submission.[3] In this case the threat produced the desired result, but it may well be doubted whether it would have the same effect in the mouth of any one but the Iron Chancellor, whose strong will dominated also the Reichstag and the throne.[4]

We now come to the Emperor.[5] The title seems to denote an hereditary sovereign of the Empire, The Emperor. but from a strictly legal point of view this is peror. not his position. He is simply the King of Prussia, and he enjoys his imperial prerogatives by virtue of his royal office. There is, in fact, no imperial crown, and the right to have her King bear the title, and exercise the functions of Emperor, is really one of the special privileges of Prussia. The language of the constitution is: "The presidency of the union belongs

[1] This was notably true in the case of the *Gerichtsverfassunggesetz* in 1873 (Blum, p. 141).

[2] See page 261, *supra*.

[3] See pages 263–64, *supra*.

[4] Lebon (p. 147) thinks that Prussia has a good deal of influence in the appointment of delegates by the other States, and refers to the case where Bismarck procured the recall of the Bavarian representative in 1880.

[5] Cf. Const. Arts. 11–19.

to the King of Prussia, who bears the title of German Emperor." The succession is therefore determined solely by the law of the Prussian Royal House, and in case of incapacity the Regent of Prussia would, *ipso facto*, exercise the functions of Emperor.[1]

It has been said that as commander-in-chief of the army and navy the Emperor has in theory the personal direction of military matters, but that in all others he acts as the delegate of the confederated governments, under the direction of the Bundesrath;[2] and even if this statement is not strictly accurate, it gives a very fair idea of his prerogatives. He has charge of foreign affairs, makes treaties subject to the limitations already mentioned, and represents the Empire in its relation to other countries, to the States, or to individuals. He declares war with the consent of the Bundesrath, and carries out federal execution against a State when it has been ordered by that body. He summons and adjourns the Chambers, and closes their sessions, and with the consent of the Bundesrath he can dissolve the Reichstag. He promulgates the laws, and executes them so far as their administration is in the hands of the Empire, subject, however, to the important qualification that most of the administrative regulations are made by the Bundesrath. He appoints the Chancellor and all other officers, except in cases where the Bundesrath has been given the right of appointment or confirmation; but it must be remembered that the laws are mainly administered by the state governments under federal super-

His power as Emperor is comparatively small;

---

[1] Laband, vol. i. pp. 202-4. [2] Lebon, pp. 154-55.

vision, and hence there are comparatively few federal officials to appoint. In short, the executive power of the central government is very limited; and even that limited power is shared by the Bundesrath.

The Emperor has, therefore, very little power as such, except in military and foreign matters. His authority as Emperor, however, is vigorously supplemented by his functions as King of Prussia. Thus as Emperor he has no initiative in legislation;[1] and indeed he is not represented in the Reichstag at all; for the Chancellor, strictly speaking, appears there only as a member of the Bundesrath.[2] But as King of Prussia the Emperor has a complete initiative by means of the Prussian delegates to the Bundesrath whom he appoints. As Emperor he has no veto, but as King he has a very extensive veto, — for it will be remembered that the negative vote of Prussia in the Bundesrath is sufficient to defeat any amendment to the constitution, or any proposal to change the laws relating to the army, the navy, or the taxes. His functions as Emperor and as King are, indeed, so interwoven that it is very difficult to distinguish them. As Emperor he has supreme command of the army and appoints the highest officers. As King of Prussia he

but as King of Prussia it is very great.

The two sets of functions strangely interwoven.

---

[1] Laband, vol. i. p. 537. Strictly speaking, the initiative in the Bundesrath belongs to the States, and in the Reichstag it is confined to the members. Laband, vol. i. p. 534.

[2] Cf. Lebon, pp. 155–56 ; Dupriez, vol. i. p. 534. If, as the German jurists maintain, the Chancellor's right to preside in the Bundesrath depends on his being a Prussian delegate, the Emperor, as such, is not represented in the Bundesrath at all. See p. 265, n. 2, *supra.*

appoints the lower officers, and has the general management of the troops over most of Germany. As Emperor he instructs the Chancellor to prepare a bill. As King he instructs him to introduce it into the Bundesrath, and directs how one third of the votes of that body shall be cast. Then the bill is laid before the Reichstag in his name as Emperor,[1] and as King he directs the Chancellor what amendments to accept on behalf of the Bundesrath, or rather in behalf of the Prussian delegation there. After the bill has been passed and become a law, he promulgates it as Emperor, and in most cases administers it in Prussia as King; and finally as Emperor he supervises his own administration as King. This state of things is by no means so confusing to the Germans as might be supposed; for it is not really a case of one man holding two distinct offices, but of the addition of certain imperial functions to the prerogatives of the King of Prussia. The administration of the country is vested in the sovereigns of the States, among whom the King of Prussia is *ex officio* president; and until one has thoroughly mastered this idea, it is impossible to understand the government of Germany.[2]

There is no imperial cabinet, and the only federal minister is the Chancellor, who has subordinates but no colleagues.[3] The reason for this is to be found partly in Bismarck's per-

The Chancellor is the only federal minister.

---

[1] Const. Art. 16.

[2] Schulze (*Preussen*, in Marquardsen, pp. 33–34) remarks that the two offices are so closely bound together that it is impossible to think of them separately.

[3] Laband, vol. i. p. 348 ; and see § 40.

sonal peculiarities, and partly in the nature of the ties that bind Prussia to the Empire. In the first place, Bismarck preferred to stand alone, and did not want to be hampered by associates. He had had experience enough of the Prussian cabinet, where each of the ministers was very independent in the management of his own department, and he did not care to create for himself a similar situation in imperial matters. After he had decided on a course of action, he hated, as he said, to waste his time and strength in persuading his colleagues, and all their friends and advisers, that his policy was a wise one. Hence he would not hear of an imperial cabinet.[1] In the second place, he did not originally intend to have any federal ministers at all. According to his plan the general supervision and control of the administration was to be exercised by the Bundesrath, while those matters — such as military and foreign affairs — which from their nature must be intrusted to a single man, were to be conducted by the King of Prussia as President of the Confederation, all others being left in the hands of the several States. The Chancellor was to be a purely Prussian officer, who should receive his instructions from the King, and be responsible to him alone.[2] This plan is very interesting, because, although in form it was not accepted, in substance it presents an almost exact picture of the real political situation, except that the power of the Prussian King has become greater than was at first

[1] Cherbuliez, *L'Allemagne Politique*, 2d ed., pp. 228–29. Meyer, in his *Grundzüge des Norddeutschen Bundesrechts* (pp. 88–97), discusses Bismarck's objections to a collegiate ministry.

[2] Lebon, p. 152.

intended.[1]   The Liberals objected to it, and under
the lead of Bennigsen the constituent Reichstag
amended the draft of the constitution, by providing
that the acts of the President[2] should be countersigned
by the Chancellor, who thereby assumed responsibility
for them, — thus making the Chancellor a federal offi
cer responsible to the nation.[3]   The principle was
excellent, but has remained unfruitful; for
the Chancellor is not responsible criminally,
and Bismarck refused to hold himself politically responsible to any one but the monarch.

He is not
politically
responsible
to the
Reichstag.

He always insisted that the motto "The King reigns
but does not govern" had no application to the House
of Hohenzollern.   In short, the parliamentary system
does not exist in the Empire, and the Chancellor is not
forced to resign on a hostile vote in the Reichstag.   If
that body will not pass one of his measures, he gets
on as well as he can without it; or, if he considers the
matter of vital importance, he causes the Reichstag to
be dissolved and takes the chance of a new election,
a course which up to this time has always been crowned
with success.[4]

[1] It is a striking fact that the high imperial officials are almost always
selected from among the Prussian functionaries.   Lebon, p. 157.

[2] This was in 1867, before the King of Prussia was given the title of
Emperor.

[3] Const. Art. 17.   Unlike matters of military administration, the acts
of the Emperor as commander-in-chief of the army are not treated as
requiring a countersignature.   Schulze, *Lehrbuch*, p. 93.

[4] I do not mean that no imperial official has ever been driven from
office by the Reichstag.   The fall of a minister may be occasionally
brought about by the opposition of a popular chamber, although there
is no general cabinet responsibility.

The Chancellor is at the head of the whole body of federal officials. Besides this he presides in the Bundesrath, and is, in fact, its leading and moving spirit. His functions. He also takes an active part in the debates in the Reichstag, where he is the chief representative of the policy of the government. But like his royal master he has a double nature, and his functions are partly imperial and partly Prussian. As Chancellor appointed by the Emperor he is at the head of the national administration, and presides in the Bundesrath; but it is as Prussian delegate that he votes in that body, and indeed his influence there is mainly due to the fact that he speaks in the name of Prussia, and casts as he chooses the twenty votes which she controls. In the Reichstag, on the other hand, he nominally appears as commissioner for the Bundesrath or as one of its Prussian members, while his importance is really due to his position as chief of the federal government.

It is obviously essential to the Chancellor's position that he should be the leader of Prussia's delegation in the Bundesrath, and should be able to direct her imperial policy. For this reason the Chancellor, except for short intermissions, has been also the president of the Prussian cabinet; and in fact the policy of combining the two offices may now be looked upon as permanent.

The powers of the German Chancellor in Bismarck's day were greater than those of any other man in the world, and his work and responsibilities were heavier than even his iron frame could His substitutes.

bear. In order, therefore, to relieve him in part, an act was passed in 1878 providing for the appointment by the Emperor of substitutes, whenever the Chancellor should declare himself prevented from doing his work. These offices were expected at first to be temporary, especially that of Vice-Chancellor, or general substitute, who was intended to act only during the illness of the Chancellor; but with the increase of business they have become a permanent necessity, the Chancellor declaring that he is prevented from doing his work by the fact that he has too much of it to do. For many years there has been a Vice-Chancellor continuously, and it has been the habit to make as many of the Secretaries of State as possible special substitutes for their own departments,[1] appointing them at the same time Prussian delegates to the Bundesrath, in order that they may be able to speak both in that body and in the Reichstag.[2] The substitutes countersign the acts of the Emperor in the Chancellor's stead, but are nevertheless subject to his orders, and thus he still remains sole head of the government, and is morally responsible for its whole policy.[3]

[1] Dupriez, vol. i. pp. 495–97. The substitution can be made only for those matters which the Empire administers directly. Dupriez, *Ib.*; Laband, vol. i. p. 358.

[2] Dupriez, vol. i. p. 522.

[3] Laband, vol. i. p. 359; Dupriez, vol. i. pp. 497–99. The federal administration began in a very simple form, for there was only one chancery office (*Bundeskanzleramt*), divided into three sections, the Prussian officials doing in some departments a good deal of federal work. But as the number of affairs to be attended to has grown, the federal machinery has become more elaborate. The general chancery office has disappeared, and there are now many separate departments, each with a secre-

The judicial branch of the imperial government remains to be considered. Justice is admin- The judi-istered in the first instance by the state ciary. courts; but curiously enough, the organization of these courts is regulated by imperial statutes.[1] Their rules of practice are also derived from the same source, for the federal government has enacted general codes of civil and criminal procedure, which apply to the state tribunals.[2] It has, moreover, enacted a universal criminal code and a commercial code, and has just added to these a general code of civil law; so that there are in each State a similar series of courts organized on an imperial plan and expounding imperial laws in accordance with imperial forms of procedure, but whose members are appointed by the local sovereign and render their decisions in his name.

Apart from administrative and consular courts, there is only one federal tribunal, called the *Reichs-* The Reichs-*gericht,* or Court of the Empire. It has gericht. original jurisdiction in cases of treason against the Empire, and appellate jurisdiction from the federal consular courts, and from the state courts on questions of imperial law.[3] It is to be observed, therefore, that

tary of state, or president of a bureau, at its head. Such are the Interior, Foreign Affairs, Navy, Post Office, Justice, Treasury, Railroads, Invalid Funds, Debt Commission, and Imperial Bank. Laband, § 41.

[1] The *Gerichtsverfassunggesetz* of Jan. 27, 1877. Laband, § 86, and see § 81. This is true only of the ordinary courts of law, the subject of administrative courts being left for the most part in the discretion of the several States. See Laband, vol. ii. p. 368.

[2] The *Civilprozessordnung* of Jan. 30, 1877. The *Strafprozessordnung* of Feb. 1, 1877.

[3] Laband, § 84.

with the completion of the system of national codes this year, the imperial tribunal has become a general court of error in all cases arising under the ordinary civil or criminal law.[1]

While speaking of the judicial branch of the government, it is interesting to notice that there
has been a great deal of discussion among
German publicists over the question whether
a court of law can inquire into the constitu-
tionality of a statute. Some writers maintain that it can do so,[2] while others insist that the promulgation by the Emperor settles conclusively the validity of a law.[3] The problem is not, of course, confined to the Empire, but may arise in the States whenever a legislature passes a law that violates the state constitution; the solution depending ultimately on the question whether

Power of the courts to hold statutes unconstitutional.

---

[1] A State which has several courts of error can create a supreme court of appeal and confer upon it the appellate civil jurisdiction of the Reichsgericht, but this has been done by Bavaria alone. Laband, vol. ii. pp. 365–66.

[2] v. Rönne, vol. ii. pp. 62–63. This was maintained as a general principle by Robert von Mohl, in his *Staatsrecht, Völkerrecht u. Politik* (1860), I. 3.

[3] *E. g.* Laband, vol. i. pp. 551–58 ; Zorn, *Staatsrecht des Deutschen Reiches,* § 7, iii. Gneist, who is commonly cited in favor of the authority of the court, came to the conclusion, in his *Soll der Richter auch über die Frage zu befinden haben, ob ein Gesetz verfassungsmässig zu Stande gekommen,* that the courts can decide whether an ordinance issued by the executive is within its constitutional powers, and whether a law has received the assent of the chambers as required by the constitution, but that they cannot inquire whether the substance of a law passed in proper form violates the provisions of that instrument.

The constitution of Prussia declares expressly (Art. 106) that statutes and ordinances are binding if promulgated in the form prescribed by law, and that the legality of royal ordinances regularly issued can be examined only by the chambers.

the constitution shall be treated as a law of superior obligation, or whether it shall be regarded merely as establishing a rule for the guidance of the legislator.

The matter, however, is one in which practice is far more important than abstract theory, and it is certain that the courts have not in fact exercised any general power of refusing to apply statutes on constitutional grounds. The late Brinton Coxe, in his compilation on "Judicial Power and Unconstitutional Legislation," has collected the most important German cases on the subject.[1] In one of these the Hanseatic Court of Appeal held in 1875 that a statute enacted in Bremen, which deprived a person of property without compensation, was in conflict with the constitution of the city, and that the court must regard the latter as a binding law and refuse to apply the statute.[2] Eight years later the doctrine of this case was expressly overruled by the federal court in another suit that arose in Bremen upon a similar state of facts, the court declaring that the constitutional provision was to be understood only as a rule for the legislative power to interpret.[3] Since that time no German tribunal appears to have held a statute unconstitutional, but in 1889 the federal court remarked, in the course of an opinion, that the question whether the judiciary had a right to examine the constitutionality of an imperial law was still an open one, although the weight of authority was in the affirmative.[4]

[1] Ch. ix.

[2] Gabade v. Bremen, Seuff, *Arch.*, vol. xxxii. No. 101.

[3] K. and Others v. Dyke Board of Niedervieland, Dec. of the Reichsgericht, vol. ix. p. 233.

[4] Dec. of the Reichsgericht, vol. xxiv. p. 3.

As the question is the same for imperial and state laws, the remark would seem to imply a change of opinion on the part of the court. It is not at all likely, however, that the Reichsgericht will have the courage of its convictions, and venture to disregard statutes passed by the legislature of the Empire.

Even in a federal system such a power could be effectively used only where the central government was exceedingly weak,[1] or where the authority of the courts had been raised to a pitch like that which it has acquired in Anglo-Saxon countries from the prolonged judicial centralization of England. It would, indeed, seem absurd to draw a distinction between public and private law, as is commonly done in Germany, and deny to the courts the right to consider the legality of an administrative ordinance on the ground that it falls into the province of public law, and at the same time give them power to pass on the validity of a statute enacted by the legislature.

To sum up what has been said, the German Empire is a federal government of a peculiar type, in which legislative centralization is combined with administrative decentralization. The centre of gravity is to be found in the body representing the governments of the several States, and here Prussia has a controlling influence, and a veto on the most important matters. In fact, the Confederation is not a union of States with equal rights, but rather an association of privileged members, so

Character of the German federal system.

---

[1] That the courts cannot exercise such a power in a centralized State, see the writer's *Essays on Government*, pp. 40–45.

contrived that Prussia has the general management, subject only to a limited restraint by her associates. And herein there is a marked contrast between the American and German federal systems. That of the United States is based on the equality of the members; and a decided preponderance on the part of any one State would destroy the character of the union. That of Germany, on the contrary, is organized on a plan that can work successfully only in case one member is strong enough to take the lead, and keep the main guidance in its own hands; [1] for if the States were nearly equal, their mutual jealousy would effectually prevent the sovereign of any one of them from infusing a real vitality into the office of Emperor, while the control of the Bundesrath over the administration would paralyze the executive unless that body derived its impulse from a single source.

[1] Cf. Dupriez, vol. i. pp. 475–77.

𝕿𝖍𝖊 𝕽𝖎𝖛𝖊𝖗𝖘𝖎𝖉𝖊 𝕻𝖗𝖊𝖘𝖘
PRINTED BY H. O. HOUGHTON & CO.
CAMBRIDGE, MASS.
U. S. A.